LIGHTHOUSE SERIES

LOST LIGHTHOUSES

Stories and Images of
America's Vanished Lighthouses

TIM HARRISON *and* RAY JONES

The
Globe
Pequot
Press

Guilford, Connecticut

ABOUT THE AUTHORS

RAY JONES is a writer and publishing consultant living in Pacific Grove, California. He is the text author of Globe Pequot's *American Lighthouses* and all eight books in the colorful Globe Pequot Lighthouse Series as well as the coauthor of *Legendary Lighthouses,* the companion to the popular PBS series. Ray has also served as an editor for Time-Life Books, as founding editor of *Albuquerque Living* magazine, as a senior editor and writing coach at *Southern Living* magazine, and as founding publisher of Country Roads Press.

TIM HARRISON is the publisher and editor of *Lighthouse Digest* magazine, co-author of *Lighthouses of Maine and New Hampshire* and of the popular children's story coloring book, *The Littlest Lighthouse*; co-founder and partner of Lighthouse Depot in Wells, Maine, which bills itself as "The World's Largest Lighthouse Gift and Collectibles Store"; and co-founder of the Lighthouse Depot Lighthouse Museum, also in Wells, Maine. He is president of the American Lighthouse Foundation, a nonprofit organization dedicated to preserving America's lighthouse history and heritage, and has been active in the restoration of a number of American and Canadian lighthouses as well as the restoration of the gravesites of former lighthouse keepers. Promoting the preservation of lighthouses, he has appeared on numerous radio and television shows, including PBS TV's six-hour miniseries *Legendary Lighthouses* and ABC TV's *Nightline*. Through the years he has accumulated an extensive collection of historical lighthouse photographs, many of which appear in this book.

Cover and page design by Nancy Freeborn
Cover photograph of original twin lighthouses at Chatham, Massachussetts, courtesy of National Archives

Library of Congress Cataloging-in-Publication Data

Harrison, Tim
     Lost lighthouses : stories and images of America's vanished lighthouses / Tim Harrison and
Ray Jones. — 1st ed.
         p.   cm.
     Includes bibliographical references and index.
     ISBN 0-7627-0443-8
     1. Lighthouses—United States—History. I. Jones, Ray, 1948–. II. Title.
VK1023.H37   1999
387.1'55'0973—dc21   99-37596
                                              CIP

Manufactured in the United States of America
First Edition/Third Printing

CONTENTS

Before the collapse of the 150-year-old Cape Henlopen Lighthouse in 1926, erosion had brought the bluff right to the edge of its tower. Notice the bulwark on the beach, placed years earlier in a vain attempt to halt the seaward flow of sand.

INTRODUCTION

Seamen love to tell the story of an old schooner captain who followed the beacon of a lighthouse that no longer existed. One especially murky evening, the captain's vessel was caught in a storm a few miles off the New England coast. Although blinded by the heavy weather and pitch darkness, he decided to make a run for the calmer waters of a small, nearby harbor. The approaches to the harbor were strewn with rocks and dangerous shoals, but the captain managed to avoid all these obstacles, and before long, his schooner was riding safely at anchor.

Astonished by this display of skill, the schooner's young first mate asked his skipper how he had managed to navigate in such terrible conditions.

"Nothin' to it," the captain replied. "I just took hold of the lighthouse beacon and followed her right in."

The first mate reminded him that the lighthouse guarding this harbor had collapsed and fallen into the sea many years earlier.

"Makes no difference at all," snapped the aging mariner. "I've been sailing these waters since before you were born, and I remember right where that lighthouse used to stand."

This delightful and rather funny sailor's yarn illustrates an important theme of this book, namely, that lighthouses have the power to guide and inspire even long after their towers have fallen and their beacons shine no more.

GHOST LIGHTS ON THE HORIZON

Lighthouses rank among our most enduring structures. Generations come and go, wars are fought and won or lost, port cities bustle and then fall onto hard times, shipping channels are dredged only to be silted over and abandoned, clever devices are invented and later replaced by new technologies, and through it all, light towers stand tall. Year after year they continue to do the job for which they were built, that of guiding ships, saving lives, and stimulating commerce. Many of the lighthouses we enjoy seeing when we go to the beach each summer were also appreciated by our grandparents and great grandparents. Some of the very same beacons that guided eighteenth-century sailing ships and nineteenth-century steamers now guide sleek ferries and nuclear-powered submarines. And yet, like everything built by humans, lighthouses cannot stand forever. Eventually they fall victim to natural or man-made calamities—or to time itself. Just like people, lighthouses will, in time, grow old and die.

Memories—and a few old photographs—are all that remain of many of America's most historic lighthouses. During the last three centuries, more than 1,600 lighthouses were built to mark our nation's Atlantic, Gulf, Pacific, and Great Lakes shores. More than half that number are now gone forever. Some were destroyed by nature, whereas others fell victim to war. But most were intentionally demolished to make way for new lighthouses or simply to get them out of the way.

By necessity lighthouses are located in exposed places. Like ships at sea, they take a constant beating from wind and water. Unlike ships, they are rooted to one spot, and when storms rush in from the ocean, they cannot run for the nearest calm harbor. They must stay where they are and take whatever the weather and the sea throw at them. For some light towers the pounding becomes too much, and they topple over.

Erosion, too, is a threat. Strong currents can cut away the very ground from under a light station. Over the years shifting sands may move the shore miles from its original location, leaving a light tower awash in the tides, dooming it to ruin and eventual collapse. When lighthouses are besieged by erosion, government and private agencies may try desperately to defend them with seawalls, breakwaters, groins, and tons of riprap, but these are only temporary, stopgap measures. The ocean never tires, never sleeps, and never faces budget shortages, and in the end, it always wins.

By far the greatest enemy of lighthouses, however, is a process some choose to call progress. Once the development of electronic timers and relays had made it possible to switch lighthouse beacons on and off automatically, the Coast Guard began to cut its costs by removing the full-time keepers from light stations. Doors were locked, windows were boarded up, and the old towers and residences were left with no one to look after them. Not surprisingly, most automated lighthouses rapidly deteriorated—some beyond recovery.

At the same time commercial and military ships have become far less reliant on lighthouse beacons. Guided by radar and by signals from satellites—also known as "lighthouses in the sky"—mariners can now plot their positions with pinpoint accuracy. Since lighthouses are no longer essential for navigation, they are not a priority item in the Coast Guard budget. Often, damaged lighthouses are not repaired. Fallen towers are rarely rebuilt.

Fortunately, public interest in historic structures has burgeoned in recent years. Local and national preservationist groups have fought hard to save what is left of America's lighthouse heritage. The responsibility for upkeep of many lighthouses has been passed along to local communities and private groups who regard these fine old buildings as monuments to our nation's rich maritime history as well as to the bravery and diligence of former keepers.

But what of the lighthouses that have already disappeared? Are these lost lights to be forgotten? No. They, too, are monuments, their towers soaring skyward and their lights burning bright, if only in memory.

AN OLD REVOLUTIONARY WAR SOLDIER FADES AWAY

Some fallen lighthouses played far too important a role in our nation's history to be forgotten. One such was Cape Henlopen Lighthouse in Delaware.

The lighthouse that once stood on Cape Henlopen at the mouth of the strategic Delaware Bay was among the earliest light towers built in the original thirteen colonies. Five earlier light stations had been commissioned by colonial or local officials. These included the Sandy Hook Lighthouse (1764) in New Jersey, the New London Lighthouse (1760) in Connecticut, the Beavertail Lighthouse (1749) in Rhode Island, the Brant Point Lighthouse (1746) on Nantucket Island, and the granddaddy of them all, the Boston Harbor Lighthouse. The stone tower built on Boston's Little Brewster Island in 1716 was the first lighthouse in North America and the first to fall in battle. After some sixty years of service, it was blown up by the British as they retreated from Boston during the Revolutionary War. Completed in 1765, the Cape Henlopen Lighthouse also came under attack by the

British during the Revolution, but it was destined to survive and serve mariners for more than a century and a half.

Like many early American light stations, the Cape Henlopen Lighthouse was intended to attract commerce. It was financed and operated, not by the people of Delaware, but rather, by those of Pennsylvania. Wealthy Philadelphia merchants were making handsome profits on sea trade that reached their wharves by way of the Delaware Bay and Delaware River. To make the approaches to their city as safe, easy, and inviting as possible, they decided to place a beacon on the prominent cape at the entrance to the bay. Funds for the project were raised by means of a lottery and of a series of special lighthouse bonds issued at 6 percent interest.

Built for a whopping 7,674 pounds sterling, a price tag considerably more than that of other eighteenth-century American light stations, the Cape Henlopen Lighthouse was made to last. Construction crews used granite brought from quarries upriver to give the tower fortresslike walls 69 feet tall and 6 feet thick at the base. It had eight interior levels, each with its own window, and a lantern room glassed in on all sides. The tower stood on a sandy hill, which boosted the lantern to an elevation of more than 115 feet above sea level. Its whale-oil lamps could be seen from up to 17 miles out in the Atlantic.

The Cape Henlopen Lighthouse soon became one of the best-known landmarks in America, and the trade it attracted further enriched the already prosperous merchants of Philadelphia. Its light had only shone for a few years, however, when relations between the colonies and their mother country began to sour. The same conflict that doomed the original Boston Light tower soon engulfed the Cape Henlopen Lighthouse as well.

During the Revolutionary War Continental forces placed a lookout in the Cape Henlopen tower to keep a constant watch for approaching British ships. Should he spot an invasion fleet, it was the watchman's duty to ride for all he was worth toward Philadelphia and spread the warning made famous by Paul Revere: "The British are coming!" But instead of swooping down on the Delaware Bay with an invading armada, the British chose to harass the colonists instead and blockade the bay with a small flotilla of warships.

In 1777 the *Roebuck,* a British frigate running low on supplies, dropped anchor just off the cape. The captain sent a foraging party ashore with orders to purchase some cattle to feed his hungry crew. The Cape Henlopen keeper, a stouthearted patriot by the name of Hedgecock, refused to sell the British any of his dairy cows. When the sailors attempted to commandeer the beasts, Hedgecock drove his small herd into the woods and threatened to provide the British with "bullets instead of beef." Not surprisingly, Hedgecock and his flintlock proved no match for the well-armed foraging party, and the keeper had to take to the woods himself. Deprived of their steak dinners, the angry seamen set fire to the lighthouse, burning the dwelling and the wooden staircase inside the tower. The station would not be repaired and back in service until the war ended in 1783.

Nearly thirty years and a generation afterward, Americans were once again fighting the British. The War of 1812 brought yet another British blockade fleet down on the Delaware Bay. The Americans could not match the fire power of the heavy British warships but struck back by extinguishing the Cape Henlopen Light and removing all the buoys and channel markers from the bay. This proved an especially damaging broadside as time and again British vessels slammed into the rocks and shoals lurking just below the surface off the cape.

Just as they had decades earlier, the blockade ships soon ran out of meat and fresh water. Foraging parties were invariably met by a fusillade of militia bullets. Facing critical shortages, the British sailed their fleet around the cape, trained their huge guns on the small port of Lewes, and demanded supplies. The haughty Americans flung the British demands back at them in the form of musket balls and cannon shot. The British, in their turn, replied with a mighty cannonade that lasted all day. Like Fort McHenry, however, the Lewes held on, and when evening fell, the American flag still fluttered above the town. Reporting on the incident to his superiors, the proud Lewes militia commander would admit to only two casualties: "one dead chicken and a wounded pig."

With the end of the war in 1814, the Cape Henlopen Lighthouse returned to its peacetime duties, but soon the light station was locked in another battle, this time with the Atlantic Ocean itself. The struggle was to last more than a century, but it was one the lighthouse was sure to lose. The strong currents near the mouth of the bay were steadily eroding the sands of the cape, and over the years, the waves moved closer and closer to the tower.

Lighthouse officials fought back, building piers and bulwarks along the beach in an attempt to dam the river of eroding sand and even piling brush around the tower to trap windblown particles. These measures slowed the erosion but could not hold it back forever.

The Cape Henlopen Lighthouse survived right up through World War I, when the keeper doubled as a spotter on the lookout for German submarines prowling just outside the Delaware Bay. But by the 1920s it was clear the lighthouse was doomed. The platform of sand on which it had been built 150 years earlier had all but disappeared. After every storm mariners looked anxiously toward the cape to see if the tower was still there. Then, one afternoon in 1926, they looked, and it was gone. The station's demise came on April 13 of that year, a sunny day with only light winds. Shortly after noon, the tower tumbled down the bank, breaking into a heap of rubble on the beach. It is said by local watermen that shortly after the sun sets each evening, they can still see the ghostly glow of the old colonial light.

SHAKEN DOWN IN SANTA BARBARA

Less than ten months before the collapse of the Cape Henlopen Lighthouse, the sun had set for the last time on another fine historic structure—the gold-rush-era lighthouse at Santa Barbara, California. As at Cape Henlopen, the destruction of the Santa Barbara Lighthouse was caused by movement of the ground beneath its foundation, but in this case the problem was not erosion. It was an earthquake.

Located on the east side of a high thumb of rock extending southward into the sea, the graceful city of Santa Barbara is unique among California's coastal communities. Anyone who takes an evening stroll on a western beach should expect to see the sun set over the Pacific, but that is not what happens here. In Santa Barbara the sun sets over the mountains—and rises over the ocean. This geographical oddity tends to confuse early-rising tourists who may have to be reminded that they are not in Atlantic City.

The unusual characteristics of this stretch of California coast are all too familiar to the masters of vessels plying the eastward-trending Santa Barbara Channel. It is easy to get lost in these waters, to mistake north for east, south for west, and any such confusion can quickly lead to disaster. Navigators must know their precise location at all times, for danger lurks at every turn. Countless ships have been crushed along these rock-strewn shores or have been torn apart by the jagged Channel Islands a few miles to the south.

For almost seventy years mariners could look to the cliffs above Santa Barbara for guidance. While they would not see the sun rising over the city's mountains, they could see a

The Santa Barbara Lighthouse as it looked in better days.

powerful light burning there at night. One of the oldest and most historic lighthouses in all the West once stood on a mesa just south of town. Built in 1856, it was one of a string of sixteen lights established by the U.S. government along the 2,500-mile western seaboard during the years following the California Gold Rush. A small, two-story stone house with a 30-foot tower rising through its pitched roof, it was nearly identical to the Old Point Loma Lighthouse near San Diego, built one year earlier, and to several other early western lighthouses.

The U.S. Lighthouse Board paid San Francisco contractor George Nagle only $8,000 to erect the structure. He used unskilled Indian laborers and mostly local materials to complete the job, but the little lighthouse proved a solid piece of work. It stood up to nearly seventy years of wind, rain, and storm. California has violent weather, however, not just above the ground, but also below it, and the Santa Barbara Lighthouse would eventually fall victim to a subterranean storm.

Shortly before dawn on the morning of June 29, 1925, keeper Albert Weeks was thrown out of bed by a powerful shock. He had difficulty getting to his feet, for the floor under him was in motion. In fact, the very ground beneath the station was shifting from side to side. Weeks forced himself up. He knew he had to act quickly to save his family.

As a lighthouse keeper, Weeks was used to dealing with emergencies of various sorts, although never one quite like this. He was also used to getting up at all hours to tend the light. He had been born into a lighthouse family. His father had served at this same light station before him and earlier as keeper of the Point Conception Lighthouse farther up the coast. Weeks had other relatives in the Lighthouse Service as well.

By coincidence several members of the extended Weeks family had gathered the previous evening for a sort of reunion at the Santa Barbara Lighthouse. In fact, the little keeper's

This pathetic pile of rubble was all that remained of Santa Barbara's historic lighthouse after the great earthquake of 1925. Note the overturned cylinder of the stone tower and, on the left, the iron railing of the fallen lantern room. The station's fourth-order Fresnel lens (not shown) was completely destroyed.

Julia Williams served as keeper of the Santa Barbara Lighthouse for almost half a century. Born and raised in eastern Canada, she made the journey to California by way of sailing ships and of an arduous horseback ride across the almost impassable Isthmus of Panama. She took over the keeper's job from her husband, Albert Williams, soon after the station opened in the 1850s. Faithfully tending its oil lamps and polishing the Fresnel lens, Mrs. Williams never once let the light fail. It is said she left the station only three times during the many decades she served here. Twice she was away in 1899 to attend the weddings of her two sons. Then, at the age of eighty, she left for a third and final time after she broke her hip in a fall and could no longer perform her duties. She died in 1911. Julia Williams was often described in California newspaper features as the "Lighthouse Lady."

residence got so crowded that Weeks had found himself kicked out of his own house. He decided to spend the night in one of the station storage buildings, and that is where he was when the earthquake struck.

Weeks rushed outside and ran to the swaying lighthouse. The walls of both tower and dwelling were already beginning to crumble, and he could see that the building had only a few seconds left. Acting on instinct and driven forward by adrenaline, he dashed into the dwelling and herded his family through the door and into the yard. No sooner had he rescued the last occupant than the structure began to groan and sag. Moments later the heavy tower and lantern crashed down through the roof, and the walls of the residence tilted outward and collapsed.

The building was too badly damaged to be rebuilt, and it would never be replaced. Since the 1925 earthquake, other lights at Santa Barbara have helped mariners find their way through the channel, but none of these have had the grace and dignity of the old stone lighthouse on the mesa.

SWALLOWED UP BY MUD, GATORS,
AND HURRICANES

Some lighthouses, such as the historic towers at Cape Henlopen and Santa Barbara, stood for generations, but many others lasted only a few years. One of Louisiana's earliest lighthouses, the original tower on Frank's Island, began to fall apart on the same day it was completed. This may come as scant surprise to anyone who knows much about the terrain of coastal Louisiana. For millions of years the Mississippi has been in the process of excavating soil from the Midwest and dumping it in the form of a thick, gooey mud at the doorstep of the Gulf of Mexico. This has created a marshy netherworld that, except for an occasional alligator lolling in a bayou, may give the impression that it is dry land. But its appearance is deceptive. In some places the mud is so deep that some construction crews have claimed they could drive piles "all the way to China" before hitting anything solid. For this reason the lighthouses built to mark the Mississippi's maze of channels and passes had a tendency to sink. Some were swallowed up by the mud at a rate of several feet a year.

The first lighthouse built in Louisiana by the United States proved an especially poor investment. As early as 1804, just after the territory became American soil, the Thomas Jefferson administration envisioned a lighthouse for Frank's Island, at that time near the Mississippi's primary entrance. The plans drawn up for the structure by noted architect Benjamin Latrobe—he had designed the Capitol Building in Washington—were so grandiose and impractical, however, that no contractor dared submit a bid for the project. An ornate, Gothic Revival edifice, it included a palatial customs office and tall light tower fashioned of brick, timber, and stone. There was even to be a fancy marble staircase. The entire complex would weigh many thousands of tons and would almost certainly be swallowed up in the deep Mississippi mud. With no one willing to build Latrobe's architectural monstrosity on the mosquito-and-alligator-infested island, the project languished for years.

Then, into the picture stepped a man who was to become the hero of many lighthouse-construction adventures—Winslow Lewis. A

More than a million bricks, 200 tons of stone, 800 tons of timber, and more than $85,000 went into construction of the Frank's Island Lighthouse in Louisiana. Completed in 1818, its foundation immediately began to settle, and the building fell apart in a matter of days. This architectural sketch shows the tower as it was supposed to have looked.

former New England sea captain, Lewis built dozens of light towers for the U.S. Treasury Department, at that time in charge of the Lighthouse Service. Lewis told government bureaucrats that the structure Latrobe had designed was sure to fail, and quickly, but that he would happily build it for them. His price: $85,000. This breathtaking sum was far more than had ever been spent on an American lighthouse. To put the figure in perspective, consider that it was more than enough to buy three million acres of land at Louisiana Purchase prices. But such was the reputation of Latrobe and the befuddlement of U.S. officials that in 1818 Lewis's outrageous bid was approved. Later that year, Lewis and a crew of masons arrived at Frank's Island and dutifully executed the Latrobe design. Then they stood back and watched as the foundation sagged, walls tilted, masonry cracked, and the whole thing fell to pieces—all in a matter of days. Lewis submitted his bill, and horrified Treasury Department auditors had no choice but to smile and pay up.

At this point Lewis offered Treasury officials a deal they could not refuse. He would replace the lighthouse that now lay in a heap on Frank's Island with a far more practical structure for the bargain basement sum of $9,750. Lewis had the 82-foot masonry tower built and in service by the spring of 1823. Its lamps and reflectors, designed by Lewis himself, produced a light that could be seen from nearly 20 miles away. Having groped blindly for the Mississippi entrance for so many years, mariners now had a light to follow, but only

An 1873 photograph of the Dog Island Light Station. The brick tower stands on a precarious foundation of sand while the residence rests only a little more securely on elevated pilings.

until 1856. By that time the Mississippi itself had retired the station by shifting its primary channel to nearby Pass a l'Outre and rendering the Frank's Island Light totally useless.

Its keepers and lantern removed almost a century and a half ago, the Lewis tower still stands, but it is shorter than it used to be, having sunk more than 20 feet into the mud. In fact, the island itself sank, and by the 1950s it had vanished altogether, leaving the tower standing in 10 feet of water.

More than twenty years after he built the Frank's Island Lighthouse, Winslow Lewis completed another Gulf Coast light tower, this one on Dog Island, just off Appalachicola on the Florida Panhandle. This proved an even unluckier place for lighthouses than the Louisiana mudlands. Only three years after Lewis finished the job in 1839, a hurricane flood tide washed out its foundation. Despite charges that his workmanship had been shoddy, Lewis was hired to pull down the remains of the original 50-foot brick tower and replace it with an all-wood structure. The latter lasted less than a decade and was smashed to splinters by hurricane winds in August of 1851. A third Dog Island Lighthouse—this one not built by Lewis—had a brick tower and separate wooden dwelling. After only a few years of service, it was destroyed in another sort of hurricane—the American Civil War—when Union blockaders burned the station. Rebuilt one last time, the Dog Island Lighthouse was obliterated once and for all in 1873 by yet another tropical storm. After this, lighthouse officials gave up trying to mark the island.

TUCKER'S ISLAND LIGHTHOUSE FALLS DOWN

Sometimes entire towns were swept away with the lighthouses that were built to serve them. This is what happened at Tucker's Island, an old-fashioned resort on the south Jersey Shore. Beginning in 1868 and for nearly sixty years afterward, the Tucker's Island Lighthouse guided vessels along the New Jersey coast. Then, in 1927, it fell into the sea. The collapse of the lighthouse removed the last human hold on Tucker's Island, which had at one time nurtured a small but vibrant community. Soon afterwards the Atlantic swept away the island itself.

Although few persons remember it now, Tucker's Island was one of the first resorts in America, if not the world. Ephraim Morse, who settled here in 1735, decided that he could do more with the property than just raise cattle on the scrubby grass. He and his descendants operated a boardinghouse on the island, and it attracted wealthy Philadelphia sportsmen who came to the shore to hunt and fish. In time the Morse family boardinghouse was accompanied by several well-appointed hotels and dozens of handsome cottages.

The island's first navigational beacon had been the Little Egg Harbor Light, established in 1848. Hardly more than a lantern placed on top of large frame house, it went dark shortly

Although a storm in 1920 obliterated much of the Tucker's Island community, the lighthouse held on for another seven years. Then, its foundation fatally undercut by erosion, the tower and residence collapsed. Government keepers maintained the light right up until a few weeks before the building toppled. A Boston photographer happened to be on hand at the end to capture the dramatic sequence of snapshots shown here.

The structure appears stable enough in this first shot of the 1927 collapse series.

Not long afterward the building has begun to tilt seaward.

The ell breaks free while the tower and the main portion of the residence pitch forward.

The chimney falls from the roof.

The Tucker's Island Lighthouse is lost.

before the Civil War. After the war, however, Tucker's Island would receive a full-fledged lighthouse. A fine, two-story structure, it was painted white with red trim. With a focal plane about 50 feet above the water, its red, flashing beacon could be seen from 12 miles at sea.

Tucker's Island residents were quite proud of their lighthouse just as they were of their town. But time and lack of railroad access had already begun to take their toll, and by the twentieth century, the entire community had fallen into steady decline. A disastrous nor'easter in 1920 provided the final blow. Awash in the tides and undercut by erosion, the hotels and homes had to be abandoned. By 1927 the lighthouse was the last prominent structure remaining on the island. Then it succumbed as well. Today, you won't find Tucker's Island on a map. Like Atlantis, it is now buried in the ocean.

A GIANT FALLS AT SHINNECOCK

It was neither erosion nor natural disaster that felled the giant tower at Shinnecock, New York. Rather, it was the hand of man. Among the tallest light towers ever built, this titan soared 170 feet above Ponguogue Point on the north side of Shinnecock Bay. More than a million bricks brought to the point by schooner and horse-drawn wagon were needed to build the lighthouse, which was completed late in 1857. Its lard-oil light, visible from up to 35 miles at sea, first burned on January 1 of the following year.

Because of its extraordinary height, the Shinnecock tower was given an unusual design feature. Its builders knew the soaring tower would sway in the wind, so they placed a crib of stout yellow pine timbers under its stone base. It was assumed that the timbers would

The 170-foot Shinnecock tower dominates its keeper's duplex residence.

give slightly as the tower swayed and then spring back into place. Indeed, the tower remained erect and almost perfectly plum for more than ninety years. Far less durable was the supposedly wind-resistant steel skeleton built to replace the original Shinnecock tower after it was taken out of service in 1931. In place for only seven years, the steel monster was bowled over by a 1938 hurricane, which, ironically, left the original brick tower unscathed.

The historic structure was nonetheless doomed. During the late 1940s, local citizens tried but failed to raise the funds needed to save the lighthouse. In 1948 it was demolished to make way for a Coast Guard administrative center. In December of that year, a crew of seven men worked for two weeks to remove the tower. Actually, they cut it down as if it were a mighty redwood. Having sawed a wedge-shaped hole in the brick walls, they soaked the supporting pine timbers in gasoline and set them on fire. When the timbers collapsed, the tower plummeted, striking the ground with a roar that could be heard 3 miles away.

The Shinnecock tower falls to earth on December 23, 1948. Notice that the upper third of the tower has broken away from the rest of the collapsing trunk.

NAVIGATING FROM MEMORY

When a light tower falls, whatever the cause of its demise, an important link to our past is broken. A key to understanding the present is lost. A chapter of the American story is forgotten, that is, unless we take care to remember. And we must.

Whether still standing or long ago destroyed, lighthouses are monuments to a heritage we cannot afford to forget. They mark not only America's coastlines but also the powerful currents of our history. They remind us of the bravery of mariners who so often scanned the dark horizon searching for their beacons. They remind us of the selfless determination of the men and women who kept their lights burning. They speak to our very best instincts as Americans.

Lighthouses are profoundly American. They offer their guidance to all and extend a welcoming hand to peoples from every part of the globe. The Statue of Liberty is a lighthouse, and in a similar way, every American lighthouse is an emblem of our national spirit.

Ironically, the tall sentinels that have welcomed so many people to America and saved so many ships and lives are themselves now in danger of extinction. Over the last half a century, technical advances in navigation and budgetary concerns have led to the abandonment and destruction of one lighthouse after another. Some have been torn down, others have been permanently scarred by vandals, and a few have collapsed into the sea. Fortunately, many others are being restored and rescued. Civic-minded individuals and organizations all over the country are working tirelessly to save our remaining historic lighthouses, and in many cases, they are succeeding. Lighthouses have been guiding ships and sailors for at least 3,000 years. Perhaps now they are guiding all of us to a better understanding of our past and of ourselves as Americans.

The same might be said for the lighthouses that have lost their battles with time and vanished. By celebrating them in words and pictures, we keep their beacons shining. By honoring them we may very well make it easier to navigate our own future. Like the schooner captain who could remember where the beacon was even though he could not see it anymore, we will still have a light to guide us.

AMERICA'S LOST LIGHTHOUSES

The following sections contain rare photographs of more than 135 of America's most historic lost lighthouses. Accompanying the pictures are stories and information gathered from Coast Guard records, old newspaper clippings, and interviews with retired keepers. Together, the words and pictures celebrate our nation's vanished ghost lights as well as the bravery and dedication of the men and women who once kept their beacons bright.

Read on and you'll glimpse a coastal America that has all but disappeared. Many of the photographs reproduced here have never been published before. Most were drawn from the National Archives or the files of the U.S. Coast Guard. Others came from the collections of photographers lucky enough to have seen these lighthouse in their heyday. Here you can enjoy them also.

The book is organized as an imaginary journey from the far northeastern coast of Maine, down the Atlantic seaboard, along the Gulf Coast, then northward from San Diego all the way to Alaska and the farthest tip of the Aleutians, and, finally, through the Great Lakes from the shores of Ontario in the East to mighty Lake Superior in the heart of the Midwest. You'll find separate chapters on the lost lights of New England, the Mid-Atlantic, the Chesapeake Bay, the South, the West, and the Great Lakes. To make it easier for you to reference their locations on a map, the individual lighthouses within each chapter are also organized geographically.

Join us now as we travel, not just along the coast, but through time itself. Look carefully, and you may see some old friends. Read more carefully still, and you may recover memories that you never knew were your own.

LOST LIGHTHOUSES

OF NEW ENGLAND

ST. CROIX LIGHTHOUSE
Calais, Maine

An early-twentieth-century photograph of the St. Croix Lighthouse.

ONE CHILLY WINTER EVENING IN 1976, A GROUP OF JUVENILES ON THE run from the law huddled in an abandoned building on Dochet Island not far from Calais, Maine. To keep themselves warm, they built a fire. During the night a spark touched the tender-dry wood in the walls, and the old building was soon a flaming torch. Fortunately, the young people escaped the blaze—although not the law—but the fire they set consumed a century's worth of tradition. The building they had accidentally burned was the richly historic St. Croix Lighthouse.

A modest, white frame dwelling with a small lantern perched on its roof, the building itself was hardly an impressive structure, but its importance to mariners was far out of proportion to its size. Built in 1857, it had once marked the entrance to the St. Croix River, a busy commercial thoroughfare, and local watermen and river pilots looked to it daily for guidance. Even lighthouse officials in faraway Washington were constantly reminded of the station because, located hard by the Canadian border, it stood at the top of the U.S. Lighthouse Service official Light List.

Although it was one of the most remote lighthouses in the nation, most of the keepers who served here enjoyed the peace and quiet of the place. Among the last St. Croix keepers was Everett Quinn, a native Mainer and twenty-five-year lighthouse veteran. Quinn happily polished the station's lens and brass and mowed the surrounding acres of grass and hay. In 1954 Quinn retired, and three years later the Coast Guard retired the lighthouse itself. Today, it is only a memory.

AVERY ROCK LIGHTHOUSE
Machias, Maine

Located off the coast of Maine near Machias, barren Avery Rock had only enough room for a very compact residence, tower, and bell housing. Nevertheless, keepers often brought their wives and families to live with them in this exposed place. The station was automated in 1934, and the structures seen here have long since vanished.

LOCATED NEAR THE ENTRANCE TO MACHIAS BAY IN MAINE, THE AVERY Rock Light Station could hardly have been more isolated. Clinging to a barren, wave-swept rock, the small, squared-off residence and tower was not considered an attractive duty station. Even so, it was maintained by full-time resident keepers from the time it was completed in 1875 until it was automated in 1934, nearly sixty years later. Often keepers brought their families to live with them on the rock, knowing full well that they might be forced to remain there for months at a time. Violent seas could lay siege to the station for entire seasons, making trips to shore all but impossible.

In 1922 twenty-one-year-old Connie Small joined her husband, Elson, at Avery Rock, where he had just been appointed keeper. There the recently married couple made a life for themselves, but it was not one many people would have chosen. Most of the time they had only the seabirds, seals, and themselves for company. A tender made infrequent stops to deliver coal and supplies, and Lighthouse Service inspectors made occasional unannounced visits to check on the condition of the station—Elson Small was awarded three consecutive annual pennants for excellence. Every two weeks or so, when the weather was good, the keeper rowed to the mainland to buy food and other necessities, but otherwise, the Smalls were cut off from the rest of the world.

Connie Small shared the hard work of running the station and keeping its all-important light in constant operation, but she also found time to do the cooking and canning. Each morning she fried doughnuts and most evenings set a fresh cake or pie on the table. When she had free time, she wrote to pen pals on shore or walked along the shore to study or sketch the marine life.

On exposed Avery Rock the battle against the elements was never ending. Storms threw huge swells against the station, threatening to knock down the modest residence and tower. On one occasion a large wave flipped over the station boat, pinning Elson Small's legs underneath. Pushing with all their combined strength, the Smalls could not move the heavy boat. They could only hope that the rising tide would lift it off the keeper's legs before he drowned. It did.

The Smalls went on to serve at several other Maine light stations, and Elson remained in the U.S. Lighthouse Service until he reached retirement age. In her nineties Connie Small wrote a book, *The Lighthouse Keeper's Wife,* about her adventures. In it she described her lonely tour on Avery Rock as among her very best years.

CRABTREE LEDGE LIGHTHOUSE
Hancock, Maine

Maine's Crabtree Ledge "sparkplug" light. Notice the fog bell.

THE CRABTREE LEDGE LIGHT STATION OFF HANCOCK POINT IN Frenchman's Bay was an open-water lighthouse of a type often described as a "sparkplug." Built in 1890 atop a heavy caisson, the tower's metal cylinder rose nearly 50 feet above the water. Its fifth-order light could be seen from about 12 miles away. Considered structurally unsound, it was sold at auction in 1934 but fell into the bay before the new owners could take possession of their unusual property.

HENDRICKS HEAD LIGHTHOUSE

Near Boothbay Harbor, Maine

An exquisite photograph of the original Hendricks Head Lighthouse in Maine. The blurred figure near the door is probably not a ghost. Early photographs required long exposures, and restless subjects who moved while the picture was being taken were likely to appear spookily out of focus.

BUILT IN 1829, THE ORIGINAL HENDRICKS HEAD LIGHTHOUSE HAD A sturdy granite dwelling with an octagonal tower rising well above its roof. This building burned in 1875 and was replaced by the present square brick tower and adjacent wooden dwelling. Although the lighthouse was sold in 1933 for use as a private residence, its light remains in operation.

A very attractive legend is associated with this light station. It holds that, following a sharp, mid-nineteenth-century gale, the keeper noticed a small bundle floating just off shore. As the swift current swept the bundle past the station, the keeper snatched it from the tides. Inside, wrapped between two tiny mattresses, he found a baby girl. She had been set adrift by her parents shortly before the storm overwhelmed their foundering vessel, killing everyone aboard. The keeper and his wife adopted the girl and raised her as their own.

PORTLAND BREAKWATER LIGHTHOUSE

South Portland, Maine

Perhaps because of its rather odd appearance, locals referred to the original Portland Breakwater Lighthouse as the "Old Bug Light." This photograph was taken on Little Diamond Island many years after the lighthouse was retired in 1874. Apparently, playful visitors decided to give the diminutive tower a pair of eyes.

PORTLAND, MAINE, IS WELL NAMED. IT HAS BEEN A BUSTLING SEAPORT for more than two centuries. Its harbor is vulnerable to storms, however, and during the early nineteenth century, destructive gales repeatedly crushed wharves and washed sizable vessels into the streets along the city's waterfront. Eventually, maritime authorities had the good sense to protect the harbor with an extensive stone breakwater. As is the case with most breakwaters, this one presented a considerable threat to navigation, and a small two-story frame light tower was placed at its far end to warn ships and guide them safely into port. Completed in 1855, the tower was of unusual design. Its inward-sloping walls supported an enclosed, octagonal observation deck that doubled as a lantern.

Although it served its purpose well enough, the little breakwater lighthouse took a terrible beating from the weather, and in 1874 it was replaced by a sturdier structure. The task of guarding the breakwater was then taken up by a squat, ornately detailed iron cylinder no less unusual than its predecessor. Some people said the new tower looked like a giant chess rook or, perhaps, a Greek or Roman shrine. Meanwhile, the far less fancy wooden tower was moved to the Lighthouse Service depot on Little Diamond Island, where it eventually fell into disrepair and was torn down.

WHALEBACK LIGHTHOUSE
Portsmouth, New Hampshire

This early photograph shows the Whaleback Light near Portsmouth, New Hampshire, as it appeared shortly after the Civil War. An earlier Whaleback tower, erected in 1820, was crushed by winter ice. Protected by its massive granite base, this one avoided that fate only to be destroyed by a storm in 1868. A third tower was completed in 1872, and it still serves mariners.

PORTSMOUTH HARBOR LIGHTHOUSE

Portsmouth, New Hampshire

NATIONAL ARCHIVES

Built in 1803, this 80-foot-tall, octagonal wooden tower marked the harbor of Portsmouth, New Hampshire, until 1877.

DURING COLONIAL TIMES THE BRITISH ESTABLISHED FORT WILLIAM and Mary to guard the entrance to the strategic harbor at Portsmouth, New Hampshire. Each night a keeper hoisted a small lantern to the top of a flagpole on the grounds of the fort. The light helped guide vessels into the harbor.

When the spirit of revolution swept through the colonies during the mid-1770s, the fort and its makeshift navigational beacon threatened the very colonists they were intended to serve. Hearing that the British were sending ships with reinforcements for their garrison at Portsmouth, Paul Revere rode hard from Boston to warn local militiamen. The Portsmouth patriots acted quickly, seizing the fort's gunpowder stores to keep them out of British hands. This proved to have been the first overt act of the Revolutionary War. It would be followed some weeks later by Revere's more famous ride and the "shot heard round the world" fired at Lexington Bridge.

Once the former colonies had won their independence, Fort William and Mary was renamed Fort Constitution, and the state of New Hampshire soon built an official lighthouse there to mark its only port of entry. In 1889 the U.S. government took charge of the Portsmouth Station along with all American lighthouses, and soon afterward, President George Washington paid the new federal facility a visit. The president was pleased with the station but apparently not with keeper Titus Salter, a former sea captain. Titus was fired.

In 1803 a new lighthouse with an octagonal wooden tower was built just outside the walls of Fort Constitution. It was not a peaceful station because cannon blasts from the nearby fort often rattled the windows and cracked the walls. Nonetheless, the structure survived until 1877, when it was replaced by the cast-iron tower that still stands.

STRAITSMOUTH ISLAND LIGHTHOUSE
Rockport, Massachusetts

NATIONAL ARCHIVES

The Straitsmouth Island Light remains in operation, but the lovely, old wood-frame tower shown here has been gone for more than a century. Built in 1835 to guide fishing boats and granite freighters in and out of Rockport, Massachusetts, it was replaced by a brick-cylinder structure in 1896. Notice the walkway bridging the marshy ground that leads down to the tower.

MARBLEHEAD LIGHTHOUSE

Marblehead, Massachusetts

The original Marblehead Light Station with its covered walkway. By the time this late-nineteenth-century picture was taken, the station's light had been raised to the top of a steel mast.

IN 1996 THE PEOPLE OF MARBLEHEAD, MASSACHUSETTS, CELEBRATED the centennial of their impressive 105-foot light tower. Some who paid their respects to the familiar, much loved, steel giant, may not have been aware that Marblehead was once served by a light tower no taller than an ordinary two-story house. Responding to a petition drawn up in a local town meeting, Congress supplied funds for a lighthouse at Marblehead during the early 1830s. Completed in 1835, it had a wooden keeper's dwelling and a separate stone tower only 23 feet tall. An unusual feature of the station was a 90-foot-long covered walkway connecting the tower and residence. The walkway allowed the keeper to attend his duties without chilling his bones. The first keeper awarded this cozy post was Ezekiel Darling, a former gunner on the *USS Constitution,* better known as "Old Ironsides."

Eventually, the construction of larger and taller buildings in Marblehead interfered with the operation of the light. In 1883 its duties were taken over by a light placed atop a tall steel mast. Then, in 1896, lighthouse officials ordered construction of the huge steel-skeleton tower that soars above the town today.

EGG ROCK LIGHTHOUSE
Nahant, Massachusetts

A 7957 Egg Rock Light, Swampscott, Mass.

JEREMY D'ENTREMONT

A somewhat stylized postcard depiction of Egg Rock Lighthouse.

ONE DAY DURING THE SUMMER OF 1922, A LARGE CREW OF WORKMEN arrived on Egg Rock, a mostly barren island about a mile northeast of Nahant, Massachusetts. Their mission was to remove the two-story Egg Rock Lighthouse from its high perch near the island summit and lower it onto a barge for shipment to the mainland. Having decommissioned the Egg Rock Light Station some three years earlier, the Lighthouse Service had sold the building to a private individual for just $5.00. Now the new owner had come to collect his property.

At first the move went well. Workmen pried the house from its foundation with jacks and then lashed it roundabout with stout ropes to hold it securely as it was lowered down the hill. But something went wrong. A rope snapped, then another, and the building went crashing down into the sea. Thus ended the career of one of New England's most picturesque lighthouses.

The original stone lighthouse raised on Egg Rock in 1856 had been destroyed by fire in 1897. It was replaced the following year by a two-story frame residence with attached tower, and it was this structure that later fell into the Atlantic.

Over the years the Egg Rock Lighthouse had many interesting residents, but the best remembered of them was likely a Saint Bernard named Milo. This huge dog loved to fetch birds from the surf, and as a result, the keeper's table was rarely in want of fowl. Milo's loud barking was said to carry even farther than the station's foghorn.

23

DEER ISLAND LIGHTHOUSE
Boston, Massachusetts

Deer Island Lighthouse in Massachusetts.

A DEADLY SANDBAR THREATENS SHIPS PASSING THROUGH PRESIDENT Roads to the east of Boston Harbor. In 1890 maritime officials marked this obstacle with an open-water "sparkplug" lighthouse consisting of a cylindrical tower set atop a heavy iron and concrete caisson. The station stood about 500 yards off Deer Island and served until 1982, when it was supplanted by an automated light on a spindle-shaped tower.

Because of their exposed locations, offshore lighthouses were dangerous places to live and work. More than a few keepers and crewmen lost their lives while going back and forth from the mainland. In 1916 tragedy visited the Deer Island Station when keeper Joseph McCabe drowned while going ashore to help his fiancée address wedding invitations.

Despite the dangers keepers at this station could not afford to be afraid of the water, and even their pets were often on familiar terms with the harbor. During the 1930s the Deer Island Lighthouse became famous for its "fishing cat." This unusual animal, belonging to keeper Tom Small, had no fear of either water or heights and often dove from the tower railing into the waves far below. Then, the sopping feline would climb back up the iron ladder with a herring in its mouth.

24

LOVELLS ISLAND RANGE LIGHTHOUSES

Boston, Massachusetts

JEREMY D'ENTREMONT

HAROLD JENNINGS

These range lights on Lovells Island guided ships through Boston's rock-strewn harbor during the nineteenth century. Range light stations like this one used a pair of beacons to help vessels keep safely within a narrow channel. Harold B. Jennings, who lived and worked at the Lovells Island Station for many years, later wrote a book about the experience. Called A Lighthouse Family, *it can still be found at many libraries and book outlets.*

NARROWS LIGHTHOUSE
Boston, Massachusetts

A postcard depiction of Boston's "Bug Light," or Narrows Lighthouse. Notice the laundry hanging below the main platform.

THE SPIDERY LEGS OF THE SCREW-PILE NARROWS LIGHTHOUSE ON Brewster Spit in the outer Boston Harbor earned it a rather unattractive nickname. Most Bostonians knew it as the "Bug Light." Even so, nearly everyone in the Boston area was saddened when the seventy-three-year-old cottage-style lighthouse caught fire and burned to its pilings in 1929.

Built in 1856, the Narrows Lighthouse stood on a sandy spit extending more than 3 miles into the harbor from Great Brewster Island. Its beacon was intended not so much to mark the spit itself as to warn ships away from Hardings Ledge, a deadly obstacle about 4 miles out. The dangers of the ledge were such that part of the spit came to be called "Dead Man's Cove" because of the number of bodies that washed up there.

For many years the Narrows Light was kept by a woman, Mrs. Frank Tenney, the widow of a former keeper. It is said that when she had spare time or the fog bell kept her awake at night, Mrs. Tenney would sit in her rocker and while away the hours with her knitting and sewing.

The station's last keeper was Tom Small, who also took care of maintenance. One June day in 1929, Small was burning faded paint off the walls with a blowtorch and accidentally set the station on fire. Unable to snuff out the flames, he finally had to take to the water and watch the station burn. It was never replaced.

SPECTACLE ISLAND RANGE LIGHTS

Boston, Massachusetts

A series of range lights on Spectacle Island once helped keep ships in safe water as they entered Boston Harbor. These two were built in 1903 and removed during the 1940s.

Here Spectacle Island keeper John Leland Hart receives congratulations upon his retirement after twenty-one years in the Lighthouse Service.

JEREMY D'ENTREMONT

JEREMY D'ENTREMONT

LONG ISLAND HEAD LIGHTHOUSE

Boston, Massachusetts

The iron cylinder on the left was the second of three light towers marking Long Island in Boston Harbor.

A SPECTRAL "SCARLET LADY" IS SAID TO HAUNT LONG ISLAND, A 2-MILE-long finger of rock near the middle of Boston Harbor. Legend has it that she is the wife of a British soldier killed here by Continental Army cannon fire during the Revolutionary War. Perhaps Edwin Tarr, the last keeper of the Long Island Head Lighthouse, haunts the place as well. Tarr died while seated in a chair and gazing out at the blue harbor. His funeral was held on a wintry day when a thick sheet of ice covered the ground. Before the old keeper could be lowered to his final resting place on the island's highest point, the pall-bearers lost their grip and Tarr's casket went tobogganing down the hill toward the station wharf. Fortunately, the casket stopped just short of the water, and Tarr was given the decent burial that was his due.

In all, three different light towers served the Long Island Head Light Station, established in 1819. The original stone tower was eventually replaced by a more durable iron cylinder. The latter gave way to the existing brick tower in 1900.

PLYMOUTH (GURNET) LIGHTHOUSE
Plymouth, Massachusetts

The octagonal Plymouth towers as they appeared in 1885.

IN 1997 THE HISTORIC PLYMOUTH LIGHTHOUSE, ALSO KNOWN AS Gurnet Light, was lifted up and moved back 140 feet to save it from the rampant beach erosion threatening its foundation. Thanks to this eleventh-hour rescue, the nation's oldest wooden lighthouse still stands, but to history-minded visitors, the old tower looks rather lonely. It once had a twin, a sister tower that disappeared many years ago.

Plymouth was the site not just of the Pilgrim landing, but also of one of the first lighthouses in North America. Built in 1769, this colonial light station employed two separate lanterns, both positioned on the roof of its dwelling. The double light was meant to help mariners distinguish the beacon from the small lanterns that had been hung at the entrances of harbors here and there along the Massachusetts coast. In 1801 the oil supply caught fire, and the building burned to the ground. Soon, it had been replaced by another double-light system, this one consisting of two separate towers spaced about 30 feet apart. In 1843 these towers were rebuilt, this time by a pair of octagonal wooden structures connected by a covered walkway. In 1871 the power of the beacons were boosted when each tower received a fourth-order Fresnel lens.

In 1924 the Lighthouse Service decided to convert all of its multiple-light stations, such as those at Cape Elizabeth in Maine (two lights), Navesink in New Jersey (two lights), and Nausett Beach (three lights), to single-light operation. This policy was followed even at Plymouth, where two lights had been displayed for more than 150 years. As a result, the northeastern tower was torn down.

BISHOP AND CLERKS LIGHTHOUSE

Hyannisport, Massachusetts

The Bishop and Clerks Lighthouse being serviced. The purpose of the scaffolding beside the tower is not known.

IN THE EARLY AFTERNOON OF SEPTEMBER 11, 1952, A SMALL FLOTILLA OF pleasure craft bobbed in light swells south of Hyannis on Cape Cod. They were piloted by local residents and summer folk who had come to witness an unhappy spectacle—the destruction of the Bishop and Clerks Lighthouse, a familiar and beloved local landmark. Severely damaged by a storm in 1935, it had stood unused and abandoned ever since. Considered a hazard by the Coast Guard, it was now about to be demolished.

Using heavy drills, workmen had bored sixty-eight holes into the tower's granite base and filled them with sticks of dynamite. Then, shortly before 1:00 P.M., observers saw a bright flash followed by billowing clouds of smoke. Through the smoke the tower could be seen leaning to one side. Then it fell apart, its huge stone blocks tumbling into the sea.

The lighthouse was built in 1857 to mark a large rock and several smaller ones known collectively as the "The Bishop and his Clerks." Sea captains who had torn open their hulls on the ledge had other, less holy names for it. Placed directly over the ledge, located about 3 miles off Point Gammon near Hyannisport, the 70-foot tower and its fifth-order light guided vessels to safety for nearly eighty years.

Best known of the Bishop and Clerks keepers was a man named Charles Hinckley who maintained the light from 1881 until 1919, when it was automated. At 4 feet and 9 inches tall, Hinckley was said to be the shortest keeper in the U.S. Lighthouse Service. The diminutive Hinckley had been a sailor in his younger years and was able to face even the most severe nor'easter without flinching. According to Hinckley being a keeper required "lots of philosophy."

SOUTH HYANNIS LIGHTHOUSE
Hyannis, Massachusetts

This delightful nineteenth-century photograph of the South Hyannis Light Station provides a glimpse of lighthouse life at its most bucolic.

DURING THE EARLY NINETEENTH CENTURY, THE NEED FOR A LIGHT AT Hyannis was so great that local watermen hung a lamp in the window of a harborside shack. In 1848 the government decided to mark the harbor entrance with an official lighthouse. Located in the village of South Hyannis, it consisted of a squat brick tower connected to a small residence by a wooden walkway. Although the light was discontinued in 1929, much of the old station still stands. Its dwelling is now a private residence.

BILLINGSGATE LIGHTHOUSE

Cape Cod, Massachusetts

The squarish Billingsgate tower and residence look high and dry in this photography, but by 1915, the entire structure was awash.

LOCATED JUST OFF THE WESTERN SHORES OF CAPE COD, BILLINGSGATE Island was once home to a thriving community. There were more than thirty homes and businesses here, and the island had its own schoolhouse. The extensive Billingsgate anchorage was marked by a lighthouse, completed in 1856. During the mid-nineteenth century, however, the sea began to eat away at the island, which at once encompassed more than sixty acres. With each passing storm a little more of Billingsgate disappeared beneath the waves until nothing remained but the lighthouse. Finally, it, too, succumbed to erosion.

Originally, government engineers had recommended building a screw-pile lighthouse on the rapidly eroding island. Had this been done, the structure might have survived long after the island itself had vanished. But Congress opted, instead, for a more traditional brick residence and tower much like others then being built in the northeast. The station's light served mariners until 1915, when flooding forced abandonment of the property.

CHATHAM LIGHTHOUSES

Chatham, Massachusetts

Chatham Light Station as it looked before the north tower (right) was moved to Nauset Beach. Both these towers were made of riveted steel plate.

AS THE NAVIGATIONAL LIGHTS ALONG THE UNITED STATES COAST GREW in number, it became more and more likely that mariners would confuse the beacons and lose their way. To help seamen tell one from another, maritime officials decided to mark some locations with two or even three separate lights. Among the first stations to display multiple beacons was the one at Chatham on Cape Cod. In 1808 two wooden towers were built on a high, sandy bluff above the Chatham harbor. Each was equipped with the best oil lamps and reflectors available at that time, and their twin lights made it easy for sailors to distinguish them from Highland Light some miles to the north.

These first "Chatham Twins" would survive for only about thirty years. Cape Cod consists primarily of compressed dunes readily gobbled up by the Atlantic. Over the years the crumbling cliffs have destroyed or forced the removal of lighthouses all along the Cape. By 1841 the cliffs threatened the Chatham Twins, and they had to be rebuilt. The brick towers that replaced them lasted no longer and tumbled over the cliffs during the 1870s. In 1877 a pair of iron cylindrical towers were erected at a more respectable—and safer—distance from the cliff's edge.

By the 1920s the Lighthouse Service had given up on the idea of multiple lights, and one of the Chatham towers was removed. Hauled up the Cape to Nauset Beach, it took the place of a three-light beacon, the famed Three Sisters of Nauset. The other Chatham tower remains in use on its original site.

CUTTYHUNK LIGHTHOUSE

Cape Cod, Massachusetts

An early photograph of the second Cuttyhunk Lighthouse. Built shortly before the Civil War, the combination tower and dwelling served through 1891. It was replaced by a conical brick tower and separate residence, which stood until just after World War II.

IN 1602 CAPTAIN BARTHOLOMEW GROSNOLD EXPLORED CAPE COD WITH his small ship, the *Concord,* and had his crew build a fort on an island known to local Indians as "Poocutohhunkkannah." After fending off an attack by war canoes, the English departed, having decided the place was too vulnerable for settlement—or perhaps they were simply unable to pronounce its tongue-twisting name. A century afterwards, the Wampanoag word for the island would be shortened and Anglicized to "Cuttyhunk."

Storms often drove vessels ashore on Cuttyhunk. During the early 1820s lighthouse officials decided to mark the island, at that time inhabited mostly by Quaker farm families. A stone tower and residence were built for about $3,000, but the work would prove to have been done poorly. The soapstone roof leaked and the walls crumbled away. The entire structure was rebuilt in 1860, but its replacement was even leakier than the original. Keepers spent much of their time setting out buckets and mopping the floor. Yet another lighthouse was built in 1892, and much to the relief of the station keepers, its roof was relatively watertight.

The third Cuttyhunk Lighthouse served for more than half a century. It was demolished shortly after the Coast Guard closed the station in 1947. The last Cuttyhunk keeper was a man named Octave Ponsart. When he died, his family had a lighthouse carved on his tombstone.

MAYO BEACH LIGHTHOUSE
Wellfleet, Massachusetts

The original Mayo Beach Lighthouse was built in 1838 for less than $3,000. The building proved no bargain, as its roof leaked so badly that keepers spent much of their time mopping up rainwater.

DURING THE LATE 1830s TREASURY AUDITOR STEPHEN PLEASONTON ordered construction of a lighthouse to mark Cape Cod's Wellfleet Bay. Like other projects carried out under Pleasonton's strict tutelage, this one was bargain priced and accounted to the penny—the contract came in at $2,819.18. And like many of the other lighthouses built by contractors able or willing to work for the tightfisted Pleasonton, it proved far less than adequate. The station had no tower, but rather an iron lantern was placed directly on top of the steep roof of the one-story residence. Meant to be efficient—and inexpensive—the design placed far too much stress on the roof, causing it to leak freely. In stormy weather keepers and their families could rightly complain that it was raining harder inside than without.

Despite repeated attempts to fix the problem, it was not satisfactorily dealt with until a new lighthouse was built in 1881. This time, the builders placed the tower on the ground immediately beside the two-story keeper's dwelling. The iron-plated cylindrical tower stood no taller than the house. After the light was discontinued in 1922, the tower was dismantled and sold as scrap. Now a private residence, the old keeper's dwelling still stands.

LONG POINT LIGHTHOUSE
Provincetown, Massachusetts

NATIONAL ARCHIVES

Located on a beach only a few feet above the Atlantic, the Long Point Lighthouse near Provincetown, Massachusetts, was vulnerable to waves and high water. In 1838 a wooden breakwater was built to protect the station. In the antique photograph above, the breakwater does double duty as a perch for the keeper's children.

TO HELP MARINERS ROUND THE TIGHT INWARD CURL OF CAPE COD and reach the Provincetown harbor safely, the government placed a navigational station at the end of a gently curving sand spit known as Long Point. Completed in 1822, it consisted of a frame residence with rooftop lantern. In 1856 the oil lamps and reflector system gave way to a sixth-order Fresnel lens. A square tower and new frame residence replaced the original structure in 1875. Only the tower still stands.

BRANT POINT LIGHTHOUSE

Nantucket Island, Massachusetts

This stout structure served longest at Brant Point. Built in 1856, it lasted until 1901.

IF FALLEN LIGHTS SHINE IN THE MEMORY OF SEAMEN, THEN NANtucket's Brant Point must be the brightest place on the coast of North America. More than 250 years ago, the island's hardy whalers built a modest, wooden tower on Brant Point at the entrance of their bustling harbor. Completed in 1746, it was only the second lighthouse built along the entire American coast—the Boston Harbor Lighthouse, completed in 1716, was first. Twelve years later it burned to the ground. Another tower was built, and it, in turn, was bowled over by a powerful gust of wind. Subsequent Nantucket lighthouses were knocked down by storms, ruined by rot, condemned by building inspectors, pulled down by government officials, and otherwise undone so that, in all, at least ten separate light towers have stood on the point. One of them is shown here.

CLARKS POINT LIGHTHOUSE

New Bedford, Massachusetts

From the tower gallery more than 40 feet above the ground, the Clarks Point keeper blows the station's hand-held foghorn.

IN 1804 A 42-FOOT STONE LIGHT TOWER WAS PLACED ON CLARKS POINT to guide vessels entering the harbor of New Bedford, Massachusetts. The Civil War convinced the government that the harbor needed protection as well as a light, and a seven-sided granite fort was built on the point during the 1860s. Its massive stone walls eventually blocked the Clarks Point beacon, and in 1869 the lantern room was lopped off the tower and placed on top of the fort. Although this light was discontinued more than a century ago, both the decapitated stone tower and its relocated lantern still stand. Heavily scarred by vandalism in recent years, these structures have been placed on the "Doomsday List" kept by lighthouse enthusiasts.

PALMER ISLAND RANGE LIGHTHOUSE

New Bedford, Massachusetts

JEREMY D'ENTREMONT

One of a pair of range lights guiding vessels into the harbor at New Bedford, Massachusetts, the small tower rested on the supports of the Fairhaven Bridge. Placed here in 1888, it displayed its red beacon for only about three years.

WHALE ROCK LIGHTHOUSE

Narragansett Bay off Rhode Island

The massive concrete foundation of the Whale Rock Lighthouse did not save it from the infamous hurricane that swept over Rhode Island's Narragansett Bay on September 21, 1938. A tidal wave smashed the station, killing its assistant keeper. Today only the foundation remains.

VESSELS ENTERING NARRAGANSETT BAY FROM RHODE ISLAND SOUND are menaced by a deadly shoal called Whale Rock. Beginning in 1871, the rock was marked by a beacon shining from a four-story light tower. Built on a concrete base, the cast-iron tower contained a few small rooms and had portholes like those on a ship. Constantly pounded by the sea, this cold and confining structure proved an unpopular duty station for Lighthouse Service keepers. Dozens of head keepers served here over the years. One stir-crazy keeper was fired after being absent from his post for 146 days during a period of only nine months.

The last keeper assigned to the Whale Rock Lighthouse was Daniel Sullivan, who happened to be ashore on that early autumn morning when the destructive hurricane of 1938 hit Rhode Island. Unable to return to his station, Sullivan could only watch in dismay as the winds howled and the water began to rise. Sullivan feared for the safety of his assistant, Walter Eberle, and as it turned out, the keeper had good reason to be concerned. Eberle was still hard at work keeping the light burning when a storm-driven tidal wave ripped the tower from its foundation. Eberle, a father of six children, was killed, and the light station was completely destroyed. It was never rebuilt.

WICKFORD LIGHTHOUSE
Wickford, Rhode Island

The publishers of this antique postcard may have thought it depicted the old Wickford Lighthouse, but not so. Instead, it offers a heavily touched-up view of the Popular Point Lighthouse, which still stands on the banks of Narragansett Bay not far from Wickford, Rhode Island. Demolished in 1930, Wickford's original lighthouse exists only in the memories of those old enough to have seen it.

MUSSEL BED SHOAL LIGHTHOUSE

Narragansett Bay off Rhode Island

The miniature light station at Mussel Bed Shoal in Rhode Island.

SURELY ONE OF THE SMALLEST LIGHTHOUSES EVER BUILT, THE Mussel Bed Shoal Station had a compact dwelling barely large enough for one occupant. Likely, the keeper lived ashore and commuted to work. A bell tower and lantern rested on the roof. Placed on its stone pier in 1873, this diminutive lighthouse marked the Bristol Ferry Channel in Rhode Island's Narragansett Bay for more than half a century. The same 1938 hurricane that swept away several other Rhode Island lights also destroyed this one.

HAYDEN'S POINT LIGHTHOUSE

Essex, Connecticut

This antique postcard contains the only known photograph of Hayden's Light on the Connecticut River not far from Essex, Connecticut. The 21-foot-high tower and a similar one at nearby Chester were built in 1889. Both were fitted with sixth-order Fresnel lenses. Neither tower still stands.

STRATFORD POINT LIGHTHOUSE

Stratford, Connecticut

A nineteenth-century view of the Stratford Point Lighthouse in Connecticut. The 28-foot-tall wood-frame tower shown here served the station from 1821 until 1881, when it was replaced by the cast-iron cylinder that still marks the point.

BRIDGEPORT HARBOR LIGHTHOUSE

Bridgeport, Connecticut

This photograph of the Bridgeport Harbor Lighthouse dates from 1875.

FEW AMERICAN LIGHT STATIONS WERE ARMED AND READY FOR MILI-tary action, but the Bridgeport Harbor Lighthouse in Long Island Sound was an exception. To ward off attack by enemy warships during the Spanish American War, the army fitted the lighthouse with a formidable battery of 10-inch guns. As it turned out, no Spanish fleet ever menaced American shores, and the big guns, placed in 1898, never fired a shot in anger.

Built on pilings near the harbor entrance in 1871, the square, wooden lighthouse guided ships with its fixed red light for almost eighty years. By the early 1950s the structure was in such poor condition that the Coast Guard was forced to abandon it. A local lighthouse lover bought the building and planned to move it to a city park for display as a monument to Connecticut's maritime heritage. While it was being moved from its pilings, however, the lighthouse caught fire and burned.

BURLINGTON BREAKWATER LIGHTHOUSE

Burlington, Vermont

Most people do not associate Vermont with lighthouses, but the state had several light towers, most of them on Lake Champlain. This tiny wooden tower guarded a breakwater at the edge of Burlington's busy harbor.

WHIPPLE POINT LIGHTHOUSE

Lake Memphremagog in Vermont

Few people have ever heard of the Whipple Point Lighthouse or of Lake Memphremagog, which lies half in Canada and half in Vermont. The lighthouse guided water traffic on the lake during the late nineteenth and early twentieth centuries. Though only a fraction the size of Lake Champlain, about 40 miles to the west, Memphremagog is subject to sudden sharp gales. Apparently, the tower took a severe beating from a spring 1906 storm and, judging from this photograph, it was unsalvageable.

LOST LIGHTHOUSES
OF THE MID-ATLANTIC

1	Throgs Neck	6	Rockland Lake	11	Bergen Point	16	Egg Island
2	Hell Gate	7	Stuyvesant	12	Billingport	17	Cross Ledge
3	North Brother Island	8	West Point	13	Tucker's Island	18	Delaware Breakwater
4	Crown Point	9	Shinnecock	14	Brandywine Shoal		
5	Coxsackie	10	Passaic	15	Mahon River		

THROGS NECK LIGHTHOUSE
New York, New York

The Throgs Neck Lighthouse on a peaceful summer day during the 1880s. Intended to be temporary, the octagonal tower shown here served for more than half a century. Notice the sail craft headed toward New York's East River. The muzzle of a Fort Schuyler cannon can be seen on the lower left.

THE NARROW BUT COMMERCIALLY VITAL PASSAGE CONNECTING NEW York City's East River with Long Island Sound was once marked by a string of lighthouses. All were discontinued and removed many years ago, but their names—Blackwell Island, North Brothers Island, Stepping Stones, Throgs Neck, Execution Rocks—remain familiar to New York area yatchsmen and commercial pilots.

Perhaps the most important of these sentinels was the Throgs Neck Lighthouse near the entrance to the East River. A stone tower built at Throgs Neck in 1827 was torn down only eight years later to make way for construction of Fort Schuyler, which guarded the eastern approaches to New York City. The octagonal wooden tower that replaced the original lighthouse was meant to be temporary, but in this case "temporary" turned out to be fifty-five years. Eventually fitted with a sixth-order Fresnel lens, it served mariners until 1890, when the government finally got around to building a "permanent" tower.

A tall, iron-skeleton structure, the new tower turned out to be less permanent than lighthouse officials had hoped. It lasted only fifteen years. By mistake it had been built directly in the field of fire of artillery pieces at the adjacent fort. The only solution was to tear it down, and in 1905, a fourth Throgs Neck Lighthouse was raised about 700 yards to the southwest of the original site. It served until 1934, when the light was supplanted by an automated channel beacon.

HELL GATE LIGHTHOUSE
New York, New York

The workshops of the Hell Gate Lighthouse are dwarfed by the station's enormous tower.

Like an overgrown oil derrick, the nation's tallest ever iron-skeleton light tower dominates New York's Hell Gate.

WHEN COMPLETED IN 1884, THE HELL GATE LIGHT TOWER JUST OUTSIDE New York City was one of the world's tallest structures. Intended to mark the strategic Hell Gate passage linking New York's East River with Long Island Sound, it was, at 255 feet, the tallest iron-skeleton light tower ever built. Standing on just four heavily braced iron legs, it held aloft nine lamps, each generating 6,000 candlepower. Together, the lamps produced a beacon said to be as bright as the full moon. Some mariners complained that it blinded them. Although impressive, the colossal tower never proved practical as a navigation aid. After just four years of service, it was torn down and replaced by a wooden tower of far less cyclopean dimensions.

NORTH BROTHER ISLAND LIGHTHOUSE
New York, New York

Keepers lived comfortably enough at the North Brother Island Lighthouse, which remained operational until 1953. Only its rotten walls remain today.

FOR MORE THAN EIGHTY YEARS A LIGHTHOUSE ON NEW YORK CITY'S North Brother Island marked the approaches to Hell Gate and the narrows of Long Island Sound. One of several light stations guarding the strategic passages that linked the East River with the open waters of the sound, it was completed in 1869. The square, wooden residence contained a kitchen, pantry, dining room, and sitting room as well as four bedrooms and an oil storage area. The 50-foot tower rose from the front of the building and was equipped with a fourth-order Fresnel lens. Abandoned after it beacon was discontinued in 1953, the building has fallen into ruin.

The station property happened to be located adjacent to Riverside Hospital, where the notorious "Typhoid" Mary Mallon was treated and later incarcerated. Although immune to typhoid, she carried the deadly disease and spread it to dozens, if not hundreds, of New Yorkers. Mary was arrested and forcibly committed to the hospital after she refused to stop working as a cook.

CROWN POINT LIGHTHOUSE

Crown Point, New York

NATIONAL ARCHIVES

Depicted in this antique postcard is New York's Crown Point Lighthouse, which once guided vessels through the narrow reaches of lower Lake Champlain. The station was decommissioned in 1926, and its residence was torn down.

Part of the Crown Point tower was later used as the base of a memorial dedicated to French explorer Samuel de Champlain.

NATIONAL ARCHIVES

COXSACKIE LIGHTHOUSE
Coxsackie, New York

A 1901 assault by Hudson River ice floes all but destroyed this light station on Rattle Snake Island near Coxsackie, New York. Only the tower survived, but it continued to guide river commerce until 1940, when it was torn down. Shown here as it looked during the late nineteenth century, this lighthouse was completed shortly after the Civil War. It replaced an earlier tower, built in 1829.

ROCKLAND LAKE LIGHTHOUSE

Rockland Lake Landing, New York

Built in 1893, the Rockland Lake Lighthouse north of New York City soon settled into the soft mud underlying a thick oyster bed at the bottom of the Hudson River. Despite the settling and consequent lean, the tower and its beacon served river traffic for nearly thirty years.

A VITAL HIGHWAY FOR COMMERCE SINCE THE TIME OF THE EARLIEST Dutch settlers, the Hudson River is strewn with rocks and shoals. Many of these were once marked with lighthouses such as the one near Rockland Lake Landing, about 28 miles north of New York City. A caisson-style structure built in 1893, the iron lighthouse stood atop a mid-river oyster bed. As it turned out, a thick layer of mud lay beneath the oysters, and even with piles to help support it, the tower soon began to settle. Before long, it began to lean like the renowned Tower of Pisa. Even so, the lighthouse served until 1923, when it was demolished and replaced by an automated beacon shining from an iron-skeleton tower.

STUYVESANT LIGHTHOUSE

Stuyvesant, New York

The Stuyvesant Lighthouse guided boatman through a narrow channel in the Hudson River. The heavy granite pier shielded the tower and residence from high water and ice.

THE KEEPER AND HIS FAMILY AT STUYVESANT LIGHT STATION IN NEW York may never have know what hit them. The Stuyvesant Lighthouse had stood beside the Hudson River for only three years when tragedy struck in March 1832. Huge ice floes had formed a dam upriver. When it suddenly broke apart, the resulting tidal wave carried away everything in its path, including the lighthouse, the keeper, and four members of his family.

A replacement lighthouse completed in 1835 proved much luckier than its predecessor. Protected by a massive granite pier, it resisted high water and ice for almost a century. In 1902 an ice jam similar to the one that had formed seventy years earlier released a flood that drove the keeper and his family from the station. Although some furnishings and equipment were destroyed, the two-story brick lighthouse survived the flood and continued in use for thirty more years. The building was torn down soon after the station was discontinued in 1933.

WEST POINT LIGHTHOUSE
West Point, New York

West Point Lighthouse, West Point, N. Y.

An antique postcard view of the light tower and fog-signal building on the Hudson River not far from the U.S. Military Academy at West Point, New York. The tower was built in 1872, and the fog signal was added a few years after. In 1921 the wooden schooner Philip Mehrhof *smashed into the station, all but destroying the fog-signal building.*

PASSAIC LIGHTHOUSE

Newark, New Jersey

The Passaic Lighthouse on Newark Bay in New Jersey. The lantern is draped to protect the station's Fresnel lens from the sun.

ONE OF FOUR LIGHT STATIONS ESTABLISHED DURING THE NINE-teenth century to guide commercial shipping traffic through crowded Newark Bay, the Passaic Lighthouse warned vessels away from the spreading mudflats at the mouth of the Passaic River. A handsome wood-frame residence with attached tower, it stood on a 6-foot-high stone wharf. A sixth-order Fresnel lens focused its beacon. By the turn of the twentieth century, the river had changed course, and shipping no longer passed near the light or the mudflats it guarded. It was abandoned shortly before World War I and eventually demolished.

BERGEN POINT LIGHTHOUSE
Newark, New Jersey

Bergen Point Lighthouse in New York as it looked during the early twentieth century.

FOR ALMOST A CENTURY THE BERGEN POINT LIGHT GUIDED SHIPS into Newark Bay through the Kill van Kull waterway. Exposed to destructive ice floes, it was protected by a heavy stone pier. Atop the pier stood a square, 41-foot stone tower and attached dwelling. Completed in 1859, this sturdy structure replaced an earlier wood-frame lighthouse that had rotted away in just seven years. The new stone building lasted for nearly a century. It's flashing white, fourth-order light was displayed for the last time in 1948, and the building was demolished two years later.

BILLINGPORT LIGHTHOUSE
Billingport, New Jersey

The Billingport Lighthouse in New Jersey as it looked about 1897. The tower stood beside the water a short distance from the wood-frame residence. An elevated walkway connected the two buildings. Both are now long gone.

BRANDYWINE SHOAL LIGHTHOUSE
Delaware Bay off New Jersey

The screw-pile lighthouse at Brandywine Shoal (right) was about to be replaced by a cheaper and more stable caisson tower (left) when this photograph was taken, probably in 1914. The old screw-pile structure—America's first—was torn down soon afterward.

LURKING JUST BELOW THE SURFACE OF DELAWARE BAY IS A PARTICU-larly dangerous navigational obstacle known as Brandywine Shoal. As early as 1823, a light-ship was placed on station here to warn ships away from the deadly shoal. During the late 1820s the government attempted to place a pile light over the shoal, but stormy seas soon washed it away. Following this unsuccessful experiment, the lightship resumed its vigil, keeping watch over the shoal until 1850. That year, government engineers employed a rad-ical new technique that allowed them to build a durable lighthouse in open water. A forest of special piles with screw-shaped blades at the end were twisted deep into the muddy bot-tom of the bay. These provided a stable platform for a light tower.

Completed in October of 1850, the Brandywine Shoal Lighthouse stood 46 feet above sea level and guided mariners with a third-order light. To protect the structure from destructive ice floes, construction crews dumped broken stone around the foundation and added an outer "fence" of piles. This concept proved a success, and the building stood up to storms and ice for more than sixty years. It was replaced by a caisson-type tower in 1914. Screw-pile technology would later be used in construction of numerous lighthouses in the muddy Chesapeake Bay and along the Gulf Coast.

MAHON RIVER LIGHTHOUSE

Port Mahon, Delaware

The Mahon River Lighthouse in 1938, when it was still tended by keeper Irvin Lynch. Notice that the building was placed on pilings to protect it from high water.

ON DAY IN 1984 ETHEL LYNCH HOLZER STEPPED ONTO THE BACK PORCH of her house near Port Mahon, Delaware, to witness a melancholy sight. She could not hold back her tears as, a short distance across the marsh, fire consumed the Mahon River Lighthouse and, along with it, many fond personal memories. Her father, Irvin Lynch, had been keeper of the lighthouse for many years, and she had spent her formative years there. Now her childhood home was gone.

A two-story, wooden structure with a small rectangular light tower at the top, the Mahon River Lighthouse was completed in 1903. Its light warned fishing boats and other vessels away from a dangerous shoal near the entrance to Mahon River. Irvin Lynch became the station's keeper in 1912 and remained at this post until he died in 1939. About ten years later the Coast guard abandoned the lighthouse, which slowly weathered and rotted until, decades later, it was destroyed by fire.

Ethel Holzer had been two years old when her family moved into the lighthouse. As a young woman, she helped her father with the constant painting and polishing his job required. She also danced and sang with oystermen who frequently visited the residence to pay their respects. Eventually, she married one of these watermen, a man named Lewis Holzer, but in all her long life she never lived far from the lighthouse.

EGG ISLAND LIGHTHOUSE

On the Upper Delaware Bay

NATIONAL ARCHIVES

The abandoned Egg Island Light in southern New Jersey was destroyed by fire in 1950.

ON THE AFTERNOON OF AUGUST 20, 1950, OYSTERMEN WORKING THE waters of the upper Delaware Bay looked toward Egg Island and saw flames reaching toward the sky. The old wood-frame Egg Island Lighthouse was on fire, and in little more than half an hour, nothing remained of it but smoldering embers. The blaze obliterated a historic landmark beloved by generations of local watermen. Built in about 1877, the two-story wooden structure had a small lantern on its roof. Abandoned in 1935, after a small iron-skeleton tower was placed nearby, the building quickly became ramshackled. Fishermen occasionally used the old residence as a shelter and may have brought on its destruction by building a fire to warm themselves and dry their clothes on a rainy day. No doubt its dry timbers burned like matchwood.

CROSS LEDGE LIGHTHOUSE
Upper Delaware Bay

Cross Ledge Lighthouse on its granite pier.

The existing Cross Ledge tower is effective but not very attractive.

FOLLOWING THE SUCCESSFUL PLACEMENT OF A SCREW-PILE LIGHThouse atop Brandywine Shoal, engineers attempted to build a similar structure on Cross Ledge, also in Delaware Bay. Ice floes destroyed the foundation before the superstructure could be put in place, and the effort to mark the ledge was abandoned. Some twenty years afterward, maritime officials decided to try again, but this time the lighthouse was built on an ice-proof foundation of solid granite. Having put in place a granite pier weighing many tons, workmen built atop it a two-story, wooden dwelling with a mansard roof. At the very top, some 58 feet above the water, was a lantern room containing a fourth-order Fresnel lens. The station was discontinued in 1910, but the structure was not dismantled until more than forty years later. Today a very modern-looking automated skeleton tower marks the ledge.

DELAWARE BREAKWATER LIGHTHOUSES

Lewes, Delaware

The Delaware Breakwater (Strickland) Lighthouse as it looked in 1891. Notice the adjacent exchange building. These historic structures were demolished in 1960.

GENERATIONS OF MARINERS CAUGHT IN STORMS OFF THE MID-Atlantic coast have made a run for Delaware Bay where they could find shelter behind the curve of Cape Henlopen. During the nineteenth and early twentieth centuries, the government bolstered the cape's storm defences by building a series of breakwaters. These created a substantial strip of calm water providing safe anchorages for beleaguered vessels. Ships, however, must take care to avoid slamming into the low-lying stone breakwaters. Over the years the breakwaters have been guarded by a succession of light towers, and two of them still stand. These are the Delaware Breakwater Lighthouse, near the port of Lewes, and Harbor of Refuge Lighthouse, a bit farther out in the bay. Both are caisson-style structures, and both date back to 1926.

Construction of the first breakwater here began in 1828, and ten years later, a brick-and-stone lighthouse was built on its far western end. Designed by William Strickland, a Philadelphia architect and engineer, the two-story stone structure was a solid piece of work. It survived countless gales and served as a lighthouse until 1901. Even after that, it continued to be used as a telegraph office, a reporting and signal station for the Philadelphia Maritime Exchange, and by the Coast Guard for other purposes. It was finally torn down in 1960.

LOST LIGHTHOUSES

OF THE
CHESAPEAKE BAY REGION

1	Cape Henlopen	7	Mathias Point	13	Wolf Trap	19	Jordon Point
2	Lazaretto Point	8	Craighill	14	Windmill Point	20	Hog Island
3	Brewerton Channel	9	Love Point	15	Stingray Point	21	Cape Charles
4	Greenbury Point	10	Blackistone Island	16	Tue Marshes		
5	Cedar Point	11	Ragged Point	17	Lambert Point		
6	Fort Washington	12	Smith Point	18	Point of Shoals		

LAZARETTO POINT LIGHT STATION

Baltimore, Maryland

An early 1930s view of a Lazaretto Depot storage yard.

THE LAZARETTO POINT LIGHT STATION IN BALTIMORE SERVED NOT only as a navigational beacon but also as a depot for tenders supplying lighthouses throughout the Chesapeake Bay region. The light station was established in 1831 to mark the entrance to the Baltimore Harbor. Its 30-foot conical brick tower was the work of John Donahoo, who built several Chesapeake Bay lighthouses. Originally equipped with lamps and reflectors, the station received a fourth-order Fresnel lens in 1858. Five years later, at the height of the Civil War, Lazaretto Point became a lighthouse depot. In addition to materials and supplies needed for maintenance of navigation markers and light stations, explosives and other Union Army ordinance were stored here. No doubt the keeper wondered if the whole place might blow up at any moment.

Fortunately, the Lazaretto Station survived the war and remained in use as a lighthouse depot for almost a century. The Coast Guard closed the depot in 1958. By that time the old Donahoo light tower had been gone for nearly thirty years. Decommissioned in 1929, it was torn down—over the loud, but ineffectual protests of preservation-minded Baltimore citizens.

BREWERTON CHANNEL RANGE LIGHTHOUSES

Baltimore, Maryland

Leading Point Lighthouse, with its bizarre black ball, functioned as the rear-range light for Brewerton Channel near Baltimore. The station was later used as a "delousing station," where passengers on incoming ships were inspected for disease.

Located just offshore, the Brewerton Channel Front Range Light at Hawkins Point was a screw-pile structure.

FOR MANY YEARS AFTER THE ESTABLISHMENT OF THE BREWERTON Channel Range Lights in 1868, vessels could follow their bright beacons directly into Baltimore Harbor. Mariners could keep safely within the narrow harbor approach channel by sighting on the Brewerton lights and keeping them in precise perpendicular alignment. The upper, or "rear range," light was located on Leading Point. The lower, or "front range," light stood some distance away on Hawkins Point. At Leading Point a large black ball soared above the light tower. Passing ships used it as a daymark. The ball and both lighthouses are now gone.

GREENBURY POINT LIGHTHOUSE
Annapolis, Maryland

A nineteenth-century view of the Greenbury Point Lighthouse.

SITUATED ON THE BANKS OF THE SEVERN RIVER DIRECTLY ACROSS from the U.S. Naval Academy in Annapolis, Maryland, the Greenbury Point Lighthouse guided watercraft from 1849 until 1934. A unique feature of the building was its wood-shingled, octagonal tower rising through the center of its roof. During the station's early years, its light was produced by a lamp much like those used on railroad locomotives. Even after its optics were upgraded, the light was not strong enough to warn vessels away from the shoals of Greenbury Point, and the station was eventually abandoned in favor of an off-shore cottage-style lighthouse placed on screw piles. In time the picturesque Greenbury Point tower and dwelling fell victim to erosion.

CEDAR POINT LIGHTHOUSE
Solomons, Maryland

This dramatic photograph shows what time and water can do to an abandoned lighthouse.

A LOW-LYING PENINSULA ONCE STRETCHED SEVERAL HUNDRED YARDS into the Chesapeake Bay from Cedar Point near the mouth of the Patuxent River. Over the years the bay slowly encroached on this narrow strip, eventually inundating it. Along with the peninsula the Chesapeake also took possession of the Cedar Point Lighthouse.

Built in 1896 to mark the river entrance, the Cedar Point Station consisted of a three-story wood-and-brick keeper's residence with a square tower attached to one corner. A fourth-order Fresnel lens focused the light, which flashed red at five-second intervals. In foggy weather the station's ear-numbing fog bell rang twice a minute. By the late 1950s the rising waters of the bay had done so much damage to the foundation that the building had to be abandoned. In 1996 the remains of the lighthouse were dismantled, inventoried, and delivered to the Calvert Marine Museum in Solomons, Maryland, to be used in the building of a pavilion at the museum.

FORT WASHINGTON LIGHTHOUSE

Near Washington, D.C.

An early photograph of Fort Washington. The pole light had likely been removed by the time this picture was taken, but the bell tower can be seen rising from behind a building on the right.

ONE OF MANY LOST LIGHTS IN THE CHESAPEAKE BAY TIDAL BASIN, THE Fort Washington Light Station was never much of a lighthouse. Located on a military base just 2 miles south of Washington, D.C., it was established in 1856 to guide Potomac River traffic. Secretary of War Jefferson Davis gave maritime authorities permission to place a light at the fort but warned that it must not interfere with military operations or discipline. Perhaps to avoid rankling Davis, civilian lighthouse officials decided to put only a simple post light at Fort Washington. The lantern was hung near the end of a wharf and displayed a fixed white light. Davis went on to serve as president of the Confederacy, while the original Fort Washington pole light was lost in the mists of time. A small fog-bell tower built on the grounds of the fort serves river vessels to this day.

MATHIAS POINT LIGHTHOUSE
On the Maryland side of the Potomac River

A 1928 view of the lovely Mathias Point Lighthouse in Maryland.

ABOUT 50 MILES UP THE POTOMAC FROM THE CHESAPEAKE BAY, VESSELS confront a sharp bend in the river. A swirling current and uncertain channel make this a dangerous place for vessels. To help them find their way, the government placed a lighthouse in open water just off Mathias Point. Built in 1876, it stood on screw piles and had a hexagonal superstructure. It guided ships with a fifth-order Fresnel lens. Unlike many other cottage-style lighthouses in the Chesapeake region, this one had no dormers. Instead, it had a second level with several windows. This gave it the appearance of a wedding cake with stepped upper layers. Although recognized by some people as one of America's most beautiful lighthouses, it was demolished in 1963.

CRAIGHILL REAR RANGE LIGHTHOUSE
On the Chesapeake Bay near Hart Island, Maryland

This idealized artist's conception depicts the Craighill Rear Range Lighthouse near Maryland's Hart Island. The extraordinary nineteenth-century brick-and-steel skeleton tower still stands, but the handsome dwelling at the base was removed in 1938. Crews lived at the station full-time until the beacon was automated in 1923.

LOVE POINT LIGHTHOUSE
Maryland Eastern Shore

As if afloat on an iceberg, the Love Point Lighthouse is besieged by ice and snow during the winter of 1902. The steamer Holly, a Lighthouse Service tender, is anchored nearby. Ice floes were hard on open-water, screw-pile light stations like this one, built in 1872. Even so, it served mariners for almost a century before being demolished by the Coast Guard in 1964.

BLACKISTONE ISLAND LIGHTHOUSE

St. Clement's Island, Maryland

The historic Blackistone Lighthouse, shown here in fine condition during the early twentieth century, was auto-mated in 1933. Afterward with no resident keeper to look after it, the building slowly deteriorated. It was in shambles by 1956, when a fire, set by a stray U.S. Navy shell, burned it to the ground.

IN 1956 A STRAY SHELL FROM THE NEARBY NAVAL PROVING GROUND exploded near the old Blackistone Island Lighthouse and set it afire. The historic building, last of the lighthouses built by noted contractor John Donahoo, burned to the ground in minutes. Donahoo built many early lighthouses in the Chesapeake region and completed this one in 1851. The station's cylindrical tower rose through the roof of its impressive two-and-a-half-story masonry residence.

Blackistone Island looked directly across the Potomac River toward Virginia. In 1864 a small Confederate raiding party crossed the river, bent on destroying the lighthouse. Plead-ing on behalf of his pregnant wife, keeper Jerome McWilliams convinced the raiders to leave his home intact. Before retreating, however, the Confederates destroyed the station lamp and lens. Soon repaired and back in service, the facility remained in use until 1956, when it was accidentally destroyed by the U.S. military.

RAGGED POINT LIGHTHOUSE

On the Virginia side of the Potomac River

The hexagonal Ragged Point Lighthouse stood on iron legs anchored securely to piles screwed deep into the muddy Potomac River bottom.

AS EARLY AS 1835 MARINERS HAD REQUESTED—IN FACT, DEMANDED—A light to mark Ragged Point and help them navigate a tricky stretch of the Potomac. A lighthouse was built at nearby Piney Point instead, but river pilots never considered it adequate. Over the years more than a few vessels ran aground off Ragged Point. Even so, government officials ignored the complaints of maritime interests for more than half a century. Finally, in 1896, Congress voted $20,000 for construction of a lighthouse at Ragged Point, but this sum would prove woefully insufficient. In the end the screw-pile foundation and cottage-style tower and residence would cost nearly twice that much, and because additional appropriations were slow in coming, the station was not completed until 1910.

This would be the last screw-pile lighthouse built in the Chesapeake Bay region. These fragile structures had proven too vulnerable to ice and severe weather, and later Chesapeake lighthouses would be built atop heavy caissons. At first engineers had considered building the Ragged Point Lighthouse on just such a caisson but, in the end, opted for the more familiar screw-pile technique. Their choice was not necessarily a bad one. The lighthouse stood securely on its spindly iron legs for fifty years. Decommissioned in 1962, it was eventually demolished.

SMITH POINT LIGHTHOUSE
On Chesapeake Bay near the Virginia Western Shore

The Chesapeake Bay region once had many cottage-style lighthouses like this one off Smith Point in Virginia. Otherwise quite durable, these screw-pile structures were vulnerable to winter ice floes. Built in 1868, the Smith Point Lighthouse was destroyed by ice less than twenty years later.

By the turn of the twentieth century, the Chesapeake's screw-pile lighthouses were being replaced by massive caisson-style structures, such as this one off Smith Point in Virginia. It dates back to 1897.

WOLF TRAP LIGHTHOUSE
On Chesapeake Bay near the Virginia Western Shore

This cottage-style, screw-pile lighthouse marked the dangerous Wolf Trap shoal. In 1893 a large ice floe knocked it off its pilings and carried it down toward the Virginia Capes.

SNAGGED BY AN UNCHARTED CHESAPEAKE BAY SHOAL NEAR THE mouth of Virginia's Rappahannock River, the British warship HMS *Wolfe* was stranded for three long months in 1691. The hapless ship gave its name to the shoal, which ever after has been known as the Wolf Trap. To save modern ships from a similar fate, this menacing obstacle is marked nowadays by an open-water, caisson-style lighthouse, painted bright red.

During the late nineteenth century, however, a screw-pile lighthouse guarded the Wolf Trap. Completed in 1870, the hexagonal, cottage-style residence and tower stood atop ten stoutly braced pilings. Despite its sturdy underpinnings the station eventually fell prey to winter ice, the nemesis of the Chesapeake's screw-pile lighthouses. In 1893 an ice floe swept the superstructure off its foundation piles. Two keepers were in residence at the time, and they barely managed to escape with their lives. The revenue cutter *Morrill* later found the cottage and tower many miles away, drifting toward the Virginia Capes. After this incident lighthouse officials concluded that the Wolf Trap Station required a massive foundation. The caisson-style structure built here in 1894 still serves today.

WINDMILL POINT LIGHTHOUSE
On Chesapeake Bay near the Virginia Western Shore

NATIONAL ARCHIVES

The mouth of Virginia's commercially important Rappahanock River was marked for many years by a lightship. Pulled off station by the Confederates during the Civil War, it was never replaced. Instead, a lighthouse was built off Windmill Point in 1869. This screw-pile light station stood directly across from the Stingray Point Lighthouse, and together, the two beacons clearly marked the river entrance. A Coast Guard modernization program spelled the end for the Windmill Point Lighthouse in 1954 and for its neighbor about ten years later.

STINGRAY POINT LIGHTHOUSE
On Chesapeake Bay near the Virginia Western Shore

NATIONAL ARCHIVES

Like shark fins, angular rocks cut through the surface of the Chesapeake Bay a few feet from the Stingray Point Lighthouse. Probably they are part of the riprap dumped here to protect the station from ice. Built in 1858, this cottage-style, screw-pile lighthouse marked the entrance to Virginia's Rappahanock River for more than century before being dismantled in 1965. The point was given its name during the seventeenth century by Captain John Smith after a painful encounter with a stingray near the mouth of the river.

TUE MARSHES LIGHTHOUSE
On Chesapeake Bay near the Virginia Western Shore

The beautifully detailed Tue Marshes Lighthouse marked the mouth of Virginia's York River from 1875 until 1960.

LAMBERT POINT LIGHTHOUSE
Norfolk, Virginia

Listing like a leaky ship, the Lambert Point Lighthouse near Norfolk, Virginia, leans out of plumb. After the station was built, its wooden piles slowly sank into soft mud at the bottom of the Elizabeth River. Its beacon blocked by construction of a huge coal wharf, the hopelessly tilted lighthouse was abandoned in 1892.

JUST OFF LAMBERT POINT IN NORFOLK, VIRGINIA, A SHOAL JUTS INTO the Elizabeth River, a busy highway for maritime commerce. Ships entering the river in dense fog may lose their way and run aground on the shoal. In 1872 the government established a modest light station here to warn pilots of the danger. Placed on wooden piles, the building had a tendency to settle, and over the years, it leaned one way and then another. By the late 1880s the lighthouse and its stubby rooftop tower were so much out of plumb that engineers could find no way to straighten it. Abandoned in 1892, the little lighthouse eventually collapsed into the river.

POINT OF SHOALS LIGHTHOUSE
In Virginia on the Lower James River

The Point of Shoals Lighthouse marked the shallow southern shore of the lower James River. The station boats hanging from opposite sides of the building provided crew members with their only links to shore. Notice that the boat in the foreground is equipped with a sail.

ONE OF MANY SCREW-PILE LIGHTHOUSES IN THE CHESAPEAKE Bay region, the Point of Shoals Lighthouse served James River shipping from 1855 until 1933. Its hexagonal structure rested on a platform held above the water by iron legs. Like many similar open–water lighthouses, it was vulnerable to ice, and it was severely damaged by heavy floes during the winter of 1871. Soon repaired, it guided mariners for another sixty years.

JORDON POINT LIGHTHOUSE
In Virginia on the Upper James River

The two-story wooden tower at Jordon Point stood beside the James River, immediately behind the keeper's residence.

FIRST DISPLAYED IN 1855, THE JORDON POINT LIGHT MARKED A sharp bend on the James River. The strong current caused rapid erosion and forced the government to relocate or rebuild the tower at least twice. Continuing erosion finally made the station useless, and it was closed in 1927. A hurricane hit the area during the 1960s, destroying what remained of the century-old lighthouse.

HOG ISLAND LIGHTHOUSE
Hog Island, Virginia

Virginia's Hog Island Lighthouse.

THE BEACON SHINING FROM THE LANTERN ATOP THE BRICK TOWER OF Virginia's Hog Island Lighthouse helped fill a dark stretch of coast between the Assateague and Cape Charles Light Stations. Built in 1854, it was equipped with only a fourth-order lens. Lighthouse officials eventually reached the conclusion that the tower was too small and its light too weak to serve ships more than few miles off the coast. As a result, it was torn down in 1895 and replaced by a 150-foot steel tower fitted with the best available first-order Fresnel lens.

CAPE CHARLES LIGHTHOUSE
Smith Island, Virginia

A rare and remarkable photograph of the 150-foot Cape Charles Lighthouse, the second tower built on Smith Island near the entrance to the Chesapeake Bay. This picture may have been taken shortly before the tower was torn down about 1895 because the big, first-order lens has already been removed from the lantern. Notice the schooner in the background. Likely it is a lighthouse tender or construction-supply vessel.

NATIONAL ARCHIVES

VERY FEW OF THE LIGHT TOWERS THAT HAVE GUARDED AMERICA'S coasts have been grander than the 150-foot giant that once soared above Smith Island near the entrance of the Chesapeake Bay. Completed in 1864 as Civil War battles raged nearby, this huge brick sentinel held a fine first-order Fresnel lens, and its beacon could be seen from more than 20 miles away. The tower was so massive and impressive that some people may have thought it would stand forever, but it lasted for only twenty years.

An earlier lighthouse had stood nearby. Its 55-foot tower had been undercut by erosion, and the same fate eventually overtook its much larger successor as well. By 1883 the Atlantic had battered its way to within 300 feet of the foundation and was moving closer at a rate of more than 30 feet per year. As a defensive measure, lighthouse officials had jetties built, but these were soon awash. As water closed in around the tower, officials were left with no choice but to build a new lighthouse. Located a little less than a mile inland from the original site, this third Cape Charles Lighthouse has a lofty 180-foot steel-skeleton tower and a first-order lens. It still guides ships passing between the strategic Virginia Capes.

LOST LIGHTHOUSES

OF THE SOUTH

1	Wade's Point	9	Sullivans Island	17	Horn Island	25	Frank's Island
2	Cape Hatteras	10	Wolf Island	18	Ship Island	26	Barataria Bay
3	Cape Fear	11	Sapelo Island	19	Chandeleur Island	27	Timbalier Bay
4	Price's Creek	12	St. Augustine	20	Lake Borgne	28	Trinity Shoals
5	Bulls Bay	13	Cape San Blas	21	East Rigolets	29	Calcasieu River
6	Cape Romain	14	Batter Gladden	22	Point Aux Herbes	30	Redfish Bar Cut
7	Morris Island	15	Round Island	23	Bayou Bonfouca		
8	Fort Sumter	16	East Pascagoula River	24	Bayou St. John		

WADE'S POINT LIGHTHOUSE
Elizabeth City, North Carolina

NATIONAL ARCHIVES

The Wade's Point Lighthouse guided vessels into the Pasquotank River and onward to Elizabeth City, North Carolina. The two-story tower and residence, where keepers lived full-time, measured 26 feet square.

ONE OF SEVERAL SCREW-PILE LIGHTHOUSES THAT ONCE MARKED North Carolina's broad intracoastal waterways, the Wade's Point Station predates the Civil War. Completed about 1859, it stood on five stout iron legs anchored securely to the bottom of Albemarle Sound. Union troops destroyed the station in 1862, but following the war, it was rebuilt. The Coast Guard extinguished the light in 1955 and sold the combination keeper's cottage and light tower to a contractor who hoped to refurbish it for use as a private residence. While being moved to shore, the building slipped off its barge and sank in the Pasquotank River, where it remains to this day.

CAPE HATTERAS LIGHTHOUSE

Hatteras Island, North Carolina

OUT IN THE ATLANTIC OFF THE COAST OF NORTH CAROLINA, THE ocean is constantly at war with itself. Here, the steamy Gulf Stream swirls up from the Caribbean to meet the cold Labrador Current, which has pushed down a thousand miles or more from the Arctic. These two rivers of seawater, each of them mightier than the Mississippi, slam into each other with a violence that can churn up hurricane-force winds, swallow up whole ships, and reshape entire coastlines.

Long ago these titanic forces helped build the outer banks, that long, narrow string of sandy islands rising unexpectedly from the ocean 70 miles or so from the mainland. The same powerful currents that built the islands also tend to push ships much too close to them, with the result that the Carolina Banks have become a sort of maritime graveyard. At least 2,300 major vessels have come to grief here, along with many thousands more of their hapless passengers and crews. One such victim was the brig *Tyrell,* swept away with all but a single member of its crew in 1759. Another was the Civil War ironclad *Monitor,* which had only recently survived its point-blank, cannon-to-cannon face-off with the Confederate warship *Virginia.*

Congress authorized a lighthouse for the cape in 1794, but political squabbling over selection of a contractor delayed the project for years. Fighting storms, mosquitoes, and outbreaks of yellow fever, construction crews finally had the 95-foot stone tower in place by late 1803. Not tall enough to be seen from the vicious Diamond Shoals extending several miles seaward from the cape, this first Hatteras lighthouse was never considered adequate. Reporting to the Lighthouse Board in 1851, a Navy inspector called it "the worst light in the world." Following the Civil War lighthouse officials had a new, 193-foot brick tower built.

This diminutive wooden tower once helped mark Cape Hatteras, perhaps the most dangerous point on the entire U.S. coastline. Only 25 feet tall, it stood in the shadow of the Cape's soaring brick towers for more than forty years. In 1897 a hurricane knocked down the little lighthouse, and it was never replaced. There are no known photographs of the original Cape Hatteras tower that once stood nearby.

Painted with distinctive spiral stripes, it still serves as one of the nation's best-known land and sea marks. The original 1803 tower remained upright for many years. Then, about 1881, it collapsed into a heap onto the beach. Not even the rubble remains. No photographs of the original Cape Hatteras Lighthouses have survived.

CAPE FEAR LIGHTHOUSE

Near Wilmington, North Carolina

Its eight, heavily braced steel legs planted firmly on the sands of Smith Island, the Cape Fear Lighthouse rose 160 feet over the beach. Its light could reach mariners as far as 20 miles away.

It took two powerful dynamite blasts to bring the tower down when it was demolished in 1958.

AMONG THE SEVERAL IMPORTANT LIGHT TOWERS THAT HAVE MARKED North Carolina's Cape Fear River was an impressive, eight-legged, steel-skeleton structure on Smith Island. Completed in 1903, it soared 160 feet above the sea. Its lantern held a magnificent first-order Fresnel lens, which produced a light often seen from as far as 20 miles away. The heavy lens floated in a mercury bath, allowing for an almost frictionless rotation.

In 1958 construction of a lighthouse on nearby Oak Island made the Cape Fear beacon redundant. That same year the steel Cape Fear tower was demolished, but it proved more tenacious than anyone had expected. A mighty blast, generated by sixty-two sticks of dynamite, severed four of its legs but failed to bring it down. A second explosion completed the job, and the huge tower finally collapsed.

PRICE'S CREEK LIGHTHOUSE
Near Wilmington, North Carolina

The ruins of the Price's Creek Lighthouse.

NORTH CAROLINA'S CAPE FEAR RIVER IS WELL NAMED. ITS SHALLOW, constantly shifting navigable channel has claimed many ships. During the late 1840s, the government attempted to make the channel safer with a cordon of lights blazing a 25-mile length of the river that linked the port of Wilmington to the sea. These included light towers at Oak Island, Orton's Point, Cambell's Island, Price's Creek, and elsewhere along the river. With the outbreak of the Civil War, all these lights went dark, and most were never restored. During the war the 20-foot-tall Price's Creek tower was used as an observation and signal station by Confederate troops. The crumbling brick walls of the Price's Creek tower can still be seen.

BULLS BAY LIGHTHOUSE

Northeast of Charleston, South Carolina

Bulls Bay Lighthouse in 1893. Because the station was built right on the beach, its vulnerability to erosion is understandable.

THE PIRATE BLACKBEARD, SCOURGE OF THE EARLY-EIGHTEENTH-century seas, used Bulls Bay in South Carolina as a hideout. Two hundred years later the bay would be used by Prohibition era smugglers to unload illicit rum and whiskey from the Bahamas. This area, however, was used by honest seamen as well, and for more than forty years during the latter half of the nineteenth century, their vessels were guided by a small lighthouse. Built on sand at the edge of the bay, the station consisted of a modest dwelling with a short tower perched on its roof. By 1897 erosion had destroyed the facility, and in time, little remained of it but a few bricks on the beach.

CAPE ROMAIN LIGHTHOUSE
On Lighthouse Island northeast of Charleston, South Carolina

The Cape Romain towers and keeper's dwelling. The residence was torn down in 1960.

SOUTH CAROLINA'S CAPE ROMAIN CAN CLAIM NOT ONE, BUT TWO historic light towers, and both might be considered ghost lights. The first, a 65-foot, conical brick structure, was built by noted lighthouse contractor Winslow Lewis in 1828. Like many Lewis lighthouses it eventually proved inadequate, and in 1858, another, much taller tower was raised nearby. Completed only a few years before the Civil War, this second Cape Romain tower has the unhappy distinction of having been built by slave labor. A 150-foot octagonal titan, it stands on an uneven foundation and leans queasily out of plumb. Despite the lean, however, it has survived nearly one and a half centuries of wind and storm.

Both towers can still be seen rising against the horizon on Lighthouse Island, now part of the Cape Romain National Wildlife Refuge. The older of the two lacks a lantern, and its Civil War era neighbor has been out of service for more than fifty years. Both stand as mute reminders—ghosts, if you will— left over from earlier times.

The abandoned Cape Romain towers as they look today. Recently, the towers were partially restored and given a fresh coat of paint.

MORRIS ISLAND LIGHTHOUSE

Charleston, South Carolina

An 1885 view of the historic Morris Island Light Station near Charleston, South Carolina. Erosion eventually swept away the island, along with the residences and outbuildings. Now awash in the tides, the tower still stands.

FEW LIGHT TOWERS ANYWHERE HAVE CAST THEIR LONG SHADOWS over more crucial happenings than the one on Morris Island in Charleston, South Carolina. A thriving port, Charleston was already nearly a century old by the time the first official lighthouse was built here in 1767. A foundation block at the base of the tower bears the following inscription: "The First Stone of this Beacon was laid on the 30th of May 1767 in the seventh year of his Majesty's Reign, George The III."

The Morris Island Light Station and the graceful city it served survived many hurricanes and even a major nineteenth-century earthquake, but these disasters could not compare with the one that befell this region during the Civil War. The conflict began at Charleston with the firing on Fort Sumter in April 1861, and by the time the fighting stopped four

Hurricane winds and high water long ago destroyed most structures on Morris Island, such as this wood-frame assistant keeper's dwelling.

years later, the city had been all but destroyed. Among the casualties was the historic Morris Island Light tower, blown up during one of several Union attacks on Charleston.

Rebuilt in 1874, the station guided mariners with its powerful first-order light well into the twentieth century and stood silent witness to the arrival of a whole new era. The tremendous earthquake that leveled much of Charleston in 1896 failed to topple the 102-foot-tall brick tower on Morris Island. In time, however, the station would be defeated by a more subtle natural force—erosion. Little by little, the Atlantic nibbled away at Morris Island until, by the 1930s, almost nothing remained. The tidal surge of a tropical storm fin-

ished the job in 1935, carrying away the station residence and, along with it, the keeper's dog and Model T Ford.

Awash in the tides, the grand old Morris Island tower still stands, a monument to the quality of its construction. Local citizens are trying to raise the funds needed to restore the structure and protect it from further water damage.

Morris Island was also once the site of several range-light towers. Here is one of them as it appeared in 1893. Posing at the left are the keeper, his son, and a friendly family mutt.

FORT SUMTER LIGHTHOUSE
Charleston, South Carolina

This 1855 view shows a light turret rising above the thick brick walls of the unfinished fort. Notice the construction material crowding the interior parade ground. The fort was still incomplete in 1861, when it came under fire by Confederate artillery.

NATIONAL ARCHIVES

A modest light tower stands on the rubble of Fort Sumter, destroyed by Confederate guns in April of 1861.

NATIONAL ARCHIVES

SEVERAL LIGHTHOUSES HAVE STOOD AT FORT SUMTER NEAR THE harbor entrance of Charleston, South Carolina. As historians and every schoolchild knows, the historic fort was the target of the opening shots of our nation's great Civil War. These photographs show two of the modest light towers that once marked the fort.

SULLIVANS ISLAND LIGHTHOUSES
Charleston, South Carolina

The steel-and-aluminum giant on Sullivans Island near Charleston looks more like an airport control tower than a lighthouse.

This wooden skeleton tower once marked Sullivans Island. A gulf of time and technology separates it from the current lighthouse.

AT THE NORTHERN TIP OF SULLI-vans Island in South Carolina, a latter-day colossus guards the entrance to Charleston Harbor. Constructed of steel and covered in aluminum siding, its triangular column reaches more than 140 feet into the coastal sky. At the top, in a room shaped more like an airport control center than a lighthouse lantern, an exceptionally powerful optic generates a beacon that can be seen from more than 25 miles away. The automated optic seldom needs maintenance, but when it does, workmen can ride up in a speedy lift. This purely functional, thoroughly modern giant was built in 1962 at the beginning of the rock 'n' roll era.

Interestingly, an assortment of far more traditional light towers once stood on Sulli-vans Island. A wooden skeleton tower and a pair of range lights were placed here during the nineteenth century. As their distinctly old-fashioned appearance makes clear, they predate, not just rock 'n' roll, but ragtime and the "Charleston" as well.

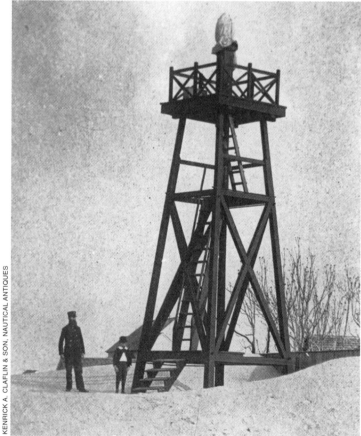

A nineteenth-century keeper and his son attend the Sullivans Island front-range and rear-range towers.

WOLF ISLAND LIGHTHOUSE
Near Darien, Georgia

An antique photograph, likely taken during the 1860s, depicts the weathered light tower on Wolf Island near Darien, Georgia. It is possible, though by no means certain, that the bearded man in the black hat is keeper William Rittenbery. Perhaps the children pictured here are his. Completed in 1822, not long after the nearby Sapelo Island Light Station was placed in service, the Wolf Island Lighthouse was blown up by Confederate forces during the Civil War.

SAPELO ISLAND LIGHTHOUSE

Darien, Georgia

The 100-foot-tall Sapelo Island tower. The open steel framework of the tower allowed gale winds to pass harmlessly through the structure. The dwellings were built on piles to keep them above storm-driven floodwaters.

COVERED WITH GNARLED COASTAL FORESTS AND ALIVE WITH WATER-birds, snakes, and alligators, Georgia's Sapelo Island is surely one of the wildest places on the eastern seaboard. It was once the home of rich sugarcane plantations, but following the Civil War, much of the island returned to nature. An important navigational station was established on the island in 1820, but unlike the plantations, it survived the war. In fact, the Sapelo Island Lighthouse remained in operation right up until 1933, its beacon guiding vessels from the open Atlantic toward the busy little port of Darien, Georgia.

The first tower built here was the work of famed lighthouse contractor Winslow Lewis. An 80-foot, conical brick-and-stone structure, it was fitted with a patent lamp and reflector invented by Lewis. Like many other such Lewis lighting systems, this one worked poorly, and it was eventually replaced with a fourth-order Fresnel lens.

In 1905 the Lighthouse Service upgraded its Sapelo Island facility, giving it a 100-foot steel-skeleton tower designed to resist hurricane winds. After the station was deactivated in 1933, the steel tower was disassembled and shipped to Michigan, where it became the South Fox Island Lighthouse. Ironically, the original Lewis tower—abandoned now for almost a century—still stands.

ST. AUGUSTINE LIGHTHOUSE
St. Augustine, Florida

This extraordinary photograph of the St. Augustine Lighthouse has been marked to show how the tower was raised over the years. The original 30-foot, wood-and-coquina structure was reinforced and raised to 40 feet in 1848. Four years later an additional 12 feet were added to the tower. Part of the building dates back to the era of Spanish occupation.

ALTHOUGH ITS HISTORY IS MURKY, THE FIRST LIGHTHOUSE IN NORTH America may very well have stood at St. Augustine, Florida. As early as 1586, Spanish settlers built a simple wooden watchtower to alert the local garrison of approaching ships. Possibly a light of some sort was placed in the tower from time to time to guide vessels through the shallow harbor. After construction of the fortifications at Castillo de San Marcos in 1695, the Spanish built a new tower. Made of wood and coquina—an oyster-shell cement— it was about 30 feet tall and was likely used on occasion as a light tower.

When the United States took possession of Florida in 1821, federal authorities had the old Spanish tower reinforced and placed in service as an official lighthouse. Originally fitted with a Winslow Lewis whale-oil lamp and parabolic reflector, the station would later be equipped with a fourth-order Fresnel lens. To give the beacon more range, the tower was remodeled and raised at least twice over the years—first to 40 feet in 1848 and then to 52 feet in 1852.

Like many other Southern beacons, the St. Augustine Light went dark during the Civil War. The tower survived the conflict and, by 1867, was once more guiding ships, but by this time, the ocean was making war on the lighthouse. Slowly but surely, erosion was cutting away the very ground beneath the building. By 1874 the tides had washed to within a few feet of the door, and that same year, the historic lighthouse was abandoned. Within months it had been replaced by the magnificent 156-foot brick tower that still serves St. Augustine today.

CAPE SAN BLAS LIGHTHOUSE

Port St. Joe, Florida

THE FLORIDA PANHANDLE IS A LIGHTHOUSE CEMETERY. FREQUENTLY raked by hurricanes, its low, sandy coastline is a neverland caught in an endless tug-of-war with the sea. Early Panhandle light stations were often built on low, sandy points or barrier islands likely to be swept into the Gulf by storm-driven flood tides. With the ground beneath them so inherently unstable, light towers here have been notoriously short-lived. Some have had to be rebuilt or moved several times, whereas others have simply fallen over like giant bowling pins.

Among the nation's least lucky light stations is the one on Cape San Blas, which juts into the Gulf about midway along the Panhandle. The Cape's first lighthouse, a brick structure built in 1847, lasted only four years. It was flattened in 1851 by the same immense hurricane that knocked down the Dog Island tower and several other lighthouses along this coast. Plagued by yellow fever, supply shortages, and terrible weather, construction crews needed five years to replace the Cape San Blas Lighthouse. They completed the job in 1856, just in time to see their handiwork blasted to rubble by a late summer tropical storm. A third Cape lighthouse fell prey to the man-made storm of the Civil War, when Confederate troops torched the entire station.

Rebuilt and back in operation after the war, the Cape San Blas Station was in trouble once again by the late 1870s. This time the enemy was erosion, and by 1880 the base of the tower was awash in the tides. Its foundation undermined by the surf, the heavy brick structure began to settle, its lantern leaning queasily over the waves. Before long it fell into the sea.

Having finally learned their lesson, lighthouse officials decided not to build another brick-and-

One of the many lighthouses built—and repeatedly rebuilt— on Florida's Cape San Blas, this brick tower fell to erosion and storm in 1882.

mortar light tower at Cape San Blas. Instead, the replacement tower would have a lightweight iron-skeleton design, allowing it to be taken apart and moved whenever it was threatened by erosion. But the station's troubles were far from over. The ship carrying the prefabricated iron tower sank in a gale off Sanibel Island near Fort Myers. Salvaged from the wreck, the tower was completed in 1885 on a site more than 500 feet from the water. Within a few years the Gulf was once more knocking on the door, and the tower had to be moved again. Over the years it would be relocated at least twice more.

BATTERY GLADDEN LIGHTHOUSE
Mobile, Alabama

The Battery Gladden Lighthouse at low tide, sometime early in the twentieth century. It was built in 1870 on the site of an old Confederate gun emplacement.

DURING THE CIVIL WAR THE CONFEDERATE ARMY PLACED SEVEN HEAVY guns on an artificial island south of Mobile, Alabama. Called Battery Gladden, the gun emplacement was intended to fight off attempts by federal gunboats to take Mobile. In the end the big cannons proved useless. Admiral Farragut's "Damn the Torpedoes, Full Speed Ahead" assault in 1864 put an end to attempts to defend the strategic port and hastened the end of the war. Several years later government engineers put the mostly dry ground of Battery Gladden to a more practical and peaceful use. There they built a lighthouse to help mariners find a key channel leading to Mobile's bustling wharves.

A screw-pile structure, like those often used in the Chesapeake Bay, much of the lighthouse was prefabricated in the north and shipped by sea to the construction site. There the hexagonal residence and tower were placed atop iron legs anchored securely to the muddy bottom of the bay. The light, supplied by a fourth-order Fresnel lens, remained in service until 1913, when improvements in channel buoys made it obsolete. The decaying superstructure remained on its perch for many years, finally collapsing into the bay about 1950.

ROUND ISLAND LIGHTHOUSE
Pascagoula, Mississippi

The Round Island Lighthouse as it looked shortly before Hurricane Georges smashed it in 1998.

ON SEPTEMBER 27, 1998, THE GULF COAST BRACED FOR HURRICANE Georges—the storm had its eye on Alabama and Mississippi. People who could leave the shore did so. Those who had to stay boarded up their doors and windows and hunkered down together in stout public buildings to wait out the blow. One aging resident of Round Island, near Pascagoula, Mississippi, however, had to face the hurricane's fury alone. This was the historic, 140-year-old Round Island Lighthouse.

With its thick brick walls, the old light tower had survived many previous Gulf storms. Ironically, the worst of them struck on September 27, 1906, exactly ninety-two years to

Leaning seaward, the massive brick base is all that remains of the Round Island Lighthouse after the hurricane. Most of the tower has been sheered off by the storm.

the day before the arrival of Georges. The early-century hurricane was one of the most powerful and deadly storms ever to hit this area. It threw a 20-foot wall of water against the station, carrying away every building except the tower. Keeper Thorwald Hansen took refuge inside the tower, where he was protected by its massive walls. He was forced to climb the tower steps to avoid the rising waters, but he survived. At least five keepers elsewhere along the Gulf Coast were not so lucky as Hansen and paid with their lives for their devotion to duty.

The Round Island tower had been built in 1859, replacing an earlier structure dating back to 1833. Focused by a fourth-order Fresnel lens, its light served mariners for the better part of a century. Then it went dark forever, in 1946, when the Coast Guard closed down the station. The venerable lighthouse had stood abandoned and alone for more than fifty years by the time Hurricane Georges bore down on it in 1998. Ironically, during the 1990s, the Round Island Lighthouse had won a new group of friends. Local preservationists were working hard to repair the dilapidated structure and restore it to its former glory. But it was not to be.

Given plenty of warning by weather forecasters, Gulf residents were well prepared for Hurricane Georges. Powerful though it was, the storm did surprisingly little damage to Pascagoula and other communities along the coast—but not so at Round Island. With only a pile of recently placed riprap to protect it from the breakers that slammed the beaches like sledgehammers, the Round Island Lighthouse stood no chance. When Georges had passed, nothing remained of the tower but a broken heap of bricks washed by the tides.

The story of the Round Island Lighthouse may yet have a happy ending. The funds originally intended to restore the old lighthouse will soon be used to rebuild the historic structure.

EAST PASCAGOULA RIVER LIGHTHOUSE

Pascagoula, Mississippi

Damaged several times by earlier storms, the East Pascagoula River Lighthouse was finally destroyed in a 1906 hurricane.

LONG THOUGHT TOO SHALLOW FOR OCEANGOING VESSELS, MISSISSIPPI'S Pascagoula River began to attract lumber and cotton freighters during the mid–1850s. Apparently, hurricane tides had scoured out a channel deep enough to turn the once sleepy town of Pascagoula into a busy port. To guide mariners into the new channel the government established the East Pascagoula River Light Station in 1854. A small combination tower and dwelling, the station was placed in the hands of Celestine Dupont, one of the nation's earliest female lighthouse keepers.

Having fallen into disrepair as it sat idle during the Civil War, the lighthouse was repaired and put back into service by 1868. In 1906 a hurricane of tremendous power struck the area and flattened the lighthouse. It was never rebuilt.

HORN ISLAND LIGHTHOUSE

Pascagoula, Mississippi

This is the second of Horn Island's several lighthouses. This one was built in 1892 and, like the others, consisted of a small cottage with a rooftop lantern.

A LOW BANK OF SAND AND SILT NOT FAR FROM THE MOUTH OF Mississippi's Pascagoula River, Horn Island refused to stay put. The island and the nearby navigable channels seemed to change locations with each passing storm. This state of affairs no doubt produced consternation among lighthouse officials who attempted to mark the island, beginning in 1874. Over the next three decades, the screw-pile lighthouse they placed here had to be relocated or rebuilt no fewer than five times. It was finally destroyed altogether by the cataclysmic hurricane of 1906. Horn Island keeper Charles Johnson was lost, along with his wife and daughter, in that same storm. Their bodies were never recovered.

SHIP ISLAND LIGHTHOUSE

Gulf of Mexico off Mississippi

Battered by storms and burned by Confederates, the original Ship Island tower stood until 1886, when it was replaced by a wooden tower.

FEW AMERICAN LIGHT STATIONS CAN LAY CLAIM TO MORE HISTORY than the one established on Mississippi's Ship Island in 1853. Part of a long chain of low, sandy barrier islands located about 20 miles from the shore, Ship Island has attracted many visitors from the sea. Among them were seventeenth-century French explorers, eighteenth-century pirates, and nineteenth-century invaders, all of whom used the island as a convenient base that provided easy access to the mainland. A huge fleet of more than 150 British warships and transports gathered here in 1814 before pushing on to press an invasion of Louisiana. The redcoats were soundly defeated outside New Orleans by General Andrew Jackson's volunteers. Otherwise, the United States might have lost the vast Louisiana Territory.

Years later another invading army made its headquarters on Ship Island. Late in 1861, Union forces drove a small Confederate garrison off the island. As they retreated, the men in gray burned the lighthouse that had been built here in 1853.

The Ship Island Light Station shortly after its new wooden tower was built in 1886. The tower was later enclosed by protective weatherboarding. The historic building burned in 1972.

An antique postcard view of the Ship Island Station.

Ironically, the Ship Island light station they destroyed owed its existence to Jefferson Davis, president of the Confederacy. Before the war Davis served in the U.S. Congress as a senator from Mississippi, and like others in Congress he worked overtime trying to secure federal facilities to boost the economy of his home state. Davis's pet project was a fort and naval base to be built on Ship Island, but he could never win an appropriation for it. Congress opted to build a lighthouse there instead. A handsome structure, it had a 45-foot brick tower and spacious keeper's dwelling, built at a combined cost of $12,000.

In time Ship Island also got a military installation, but certainly not the one Davis had wanted. By 1861 Davis had left Congress to become the Confederate president, and not long afterward, Ship Island fell to an overwhelming Federal force. As the site of Fort Massachusetts and a coaling station used by the Union fleet blockading the Gulf Coast, the island remained a thorn in Davis's side throughout the war. The lighthouse was repaired and pressed into service guiding Union warships. The windows facing the mainland were blacked out so that Southern blockade runners could not make use of the light.

The Ship Island Lighthouse took a beating during the war and suffered from several punishing storms during the years that followed. By the 1880s it literally began to fall apart. Inspectors declared the building unsafe, and in 1886, it was pulled down and a pyramidal, wood-frame tower built to replace it. Unlike most wooden buildings on the humid and stormy Gulf Coast, this one proved surprising durable, perhaps because it was covered by protective weatherboarding. It remained intact and in service right up until 1972, when it burned to the ground in a fire accidentally set by tourists. A steel-skeleton tower took its place and continues to guide Gulf shipping. A plan to build a replica of the original lighthouse is under discussion.

CHANDELEUR ISLAND LIGHTHOUSE

Chandeleur Island, Louisiana

Left leaning and awash after a late-nineteenth-century hurricane, this brick light tower on Louisiana's Chandeleur Island had to be replaced.

AN ARCH OF LOW, SANDY ISLANDS FORMS A 30-MILE-LONG WALL IN THE Gulf of Mexico to the east of New Orleans. Since 1848 a navigational light has helped guide ships around this substantial obstacle. The first Chandeleur Island Lighthouse lasted only four years. In 1852 a hurricane blasted its brick tower and forced the keeper and his family onto the roof of the dwelling, which floated away and later came to rest on a beach about a mile away.

After a second Chandeleur Island tower was all but destroyed by a tropical storm in 1893, lighthouse officials wisely opted to replace it with a storm-resistant steel-skeleton structure. Completed in 1896, the 100-foot-tall steel tower has stood for more than century.

LAKE BORGNE LIGHTHOUSE

Point Clear, Mississippi

This century-old photograph shows the Lake Borgne Lighthouse resting securely on its iron screw piles. Anchored deep in the Mississippi mud, the piles kept the station from sinking, the fate of many light towers in the region. The boardwalk in the foreground helped keepers and crewmen keep their feet out of the mud.

ALTHOUGH OFFICIALLY LISTED AS THE LAKE BORGNE LIGHTHOUSE, THIS beacon was known to local watermen as the St. Joe Light. As a matter of fact, it was built in 1889 as a replacement for an earlier light on nearby St. Joseph Island. The latter had been all but swallowed up by the island's seemingly bottomless mud.

Held above the mud by long screw piles, the Lake Borgne Lighthouse managed to avoid sinking. Its seven-room combination residence and tower lasted until 1906, when the great hurricane of that year battered them to pieces. The screw-pile foundation remained sound after the storm, and the superstructure was soon replaced. The station's fifth-order light marked Grande Pass until it was extinguished and the lighthouse abandoned in 1937.

EAST RIGOLETS LIGHTHOUSE

Southeastern Louisiana

At one time vital for freighters approaching Lake Pontchartrain and New Orleans, the East Rigolets tower stands lanternless and abandoned.

NO AMERICAN LIGHTHOUSE MARKED A WATERWAY ANY MORE IMPORtant that the one lighted by the East Rigolets Lighthouse in Louisiana. A winding bayou called the Rigolets links Lake Pontchartrain with the Mississippi Sound and the Gulf of Mexico. During the era of sail, freighters found it extremely difficult to fight their way up the Mississippi River to New Orleans. Ocean traffic could reach the city only by way of the lake, and its only access to the Gulf was through the Rigolets. For many years this vital passage went unlighted, but in 1831 Congress finally authorized a lighthouse to mark the east end of the bayou.

Completed in 1834, the East Rigolets Light Station consisted of a 45-foot masonry tower and separate keeper's residence. Years later, a government inspector would find, to his astonishment, that the heavy tower had been built without a foundation. Even so, it remained remarkably straight. For more than forty years, the tower survived the negligence of its builders, hurricanes, war, and sloppy maintenance, only to be undone by progress. By the 1870s steamers were moving up the Mississippi with ease, and a coastal railroad line carried much of the freight formerly shipped via the Rigolets. In 1874 the light station was closed and its keepers sent to tend other lighthouses. The abandoned tower crumbled away sometime during the early twentieth century.

POINT AUX HERBES LIGHTHOUSE
On Lake Pontchartrain in Louisiana

NATIONAL ARCHIVES

LIGHTHOUSE DIGEST PHOTO

Built in 1875, the Point Aux Herbes ("Grassy Point") Lighthouse on Lake Pontchartrain rested on brick pyramids rather than iron pilings. Decommissioned after World War II, it was destroyed by fire during the 1950s.

BAYOU BONFOUCA LIGHTHOUSE
On Lake Pontchartrain in Louisiana

This extraordinary early photograph shows the Bayou Bonfouca Lighthouse as it looked shortly before the Civil War.

ESTABLISHED IN 1848 TO MARK A SMALL PORT ON THE NORTH SHORE of Lake Pontchartrain, the Bayou Bonfouca Light shined for only fourteen years. It guided small freighters visiting the area to load cattle and brick for shipment across the lake to New Orleans. Built for less than $3,000, the lighthouse was not a grand edifice. It consisted of a simple, two-room wooden dwelling with a small, octagonal tower protruding 12 feet above its pitched roof. It was obvious that government officials considered the station of relatively little importance. Indeed, its construction had been delayed for several years because no one in Washington could find the bayou on a map.

The station served during a turbulent period, as the nation was marching inexorably toward disunion. The outbreak of the Civil War in 1861 doomed the little lighthouse and many others along the Southern coast. Following the capture of New Orleans by the Union in 1862, Confederate raiders burned the station and took its keeper prisoner. The keeper, a man named Vincenzo Scorza, managed to escape his captors and make his way safely to New Orleans. The lighthouse where he had served for more than a decade was never rebuilt.

BAYOU ST. JOHN LIGHTHOUSE

Eastern Louisiana

NATIONAL ARCHIVES

Established in 1811, the Bayou St. John Light marked a key waterway linking Lake Pontchartrain to New Orleans. Over the years several different towers served the station. The cottage-style screw-pile structure shown here stood from 1855 until the mid-1870s.

AMONG THE EARLIEST NAVIGATIONAL LIGHTS IN LOUISIANA WAS THE one marking Bayou St. John, a strategic waterway linking Lake Pontchartrain to New Orleans. The Spanish and French had maintained a light here before the purchase of the Louisiana Territory by the United States. In 1811 the U.S. government built its own lighthouse here, but it was a modest affair. Completed for a miserly $2,000, it consisted of a flimsy skeleton tower supporting a rather dim light, visible from only about 8 miles away.

Decades passed before the bayou received a more adequate light station. A cottage-style lighthouse perched on an elevated screw-pile foundation, it was built about 1855. The lantern rose from the center of the dwelling's sloped roof and placed its sixth-order light almost 40 feet above the waters of the lake. Repeatedly damaged by storms, it was repaired and kept in service until a powerful gale delivered the final blow in 1876. A makeshift replacement light lasted only about two years. Rendered obsolete after engineers cut a new entrance to the bayou some distance away, the station was abandoned in 1878.

BARATARIA BAY LIGHTHOUSE

Eastern Louisiana

The wood-skeleton tower at Barataria Bay in Louisiana.

THE EARLY-NINETEENTH-CENTURY PIRATE JEAN LAFITTE MADE HIS home on Barataria Bay, just west of the Mississippi Bay. The swashbuckling Lafitte had no light to help him find the bay. Nor, most likely, did he need one. Later mariners, however, sailing into the bay through barely navigable Grants Pass, were glad of the guidance provided by the Barataria Bay Lighthouse, completed in 1856. An octagonal brick tower about 55 feet high, it was built at a cost of $10,000. Darkened briefly during the Civil War, the light served until 1893, when the tower was destroyed by a hurricane. Today, little remains of the original light but a nondescript pile of brick. Nearby, an automated light atop a wooden skeleton tower continues to mark the pass.

TIMBALIER BAY LIGHTHOUSE

Southern Louisiana

A very early photograph of the 1857 Timbalier Bay tower. Pummeled by storms, it collapsed in 1886.

THE GULF OF MEXICO HAS EARNED ITS REPUTATION AS "HURRICANE Alley," and nearly every year giant tropical disturbances come spinning up out of the tropics to beleaguer one or another section of the Gulf Coast. Lighthouses are extremely vulnerable to these huge storms, which can generate energies equal to many hydrogen bombs. Established in 1857 to guide vessels through a stretch of water at one time thought unnavigable, the Louisiana Timbalier Bay Light Station seemed to invite hurricanes. Hit repeatedly during its first years of service, the station was in shambles by 1866. That summer, the keeper resigned rather than continue climbing the steps of the tower, which he believed was on the point of collapse. Shortly thereafter, it did.

115

The steel-skeleton tower on Timbalier Bay. Battered by gales and undercut by erosion, it was bowled over by an 1894 hurricane.

Abandoned and decaying, the third and final Timbalier Bay Lighthouse clings to its wooden piles for a few more hours. Later on the same day this photograph was taken in 1985, Hurricane Juan struck Louisiana. When the storm had passed, the old tower had vanished.

The second Timbalier Bay tower was a sturdier structure. Completed in 1875, it had a tall steel skeleton anchored to screw piles in open water. Although designed to withstand high winds, this tower lasted only nineteen years. Knocked this way and that by a series of powerful gales, it finally came crashing down in an 1894 hurricane.

Understandably reluctant to build another tower in this exposed location, lighthouse officials waited more than two decades before trying again. As a result, the third and final Timbalier Bay Station was not ready for service until 1917. Placed on a forest of iron-encased wood pilings, it would prove far more durable than its predecessors. Although discontinued and abandoned during the 1950s, it clung to its piles and remained intact right up until 1985, when Hurricane Juan swept it away.

TRINITY SHOALS LIGHTHOUSE

Southern Louisiana

The Trinity Shoals Lighthouse is a "ghost light" of a different sort—it was never built. Workmen struggled for several months in 1873 trying to erect the 110-foot steel tower in open water some 20 miles off the south coast of Louisiana. After a mid-November hurricane sunk the construction tender, the project was abandoned. This Harpers Weekly artist's rendering shows the station as it might have appeared, had it ever been completed.

CALCASIEU RIVER LIGHTHOUSE

Near Cameron, Louisiana

The Calcasieu River Lighthouse in 1893.

BALD EAGLES CAN STILL BE SEEN OCCASIONALLY SOARING ABOVE THE Calcasieu River about 35 miles from the Texas border. The river and the lighthouse that formerly stood here took their names from an Atakapa Indian word meaning "crying eagle." The lighthouse was built in 1876 to mark the mouth of the river, which at that time carried a lively trade in lumber.

Prefabricated in the north and shipped to the site, the 50-foot pyramidal tower was sheathed in iron boiler plate intended to protect it from the Gulf's prodigious storms. Standing on screw piles on marshy ground about 3 miles from the river entrance, the Calcasieu River Lighthouse guided freighters with a fourth-order Fresnel lens. The tower's iron walls were tested by more than one hurricane, most notably in 1886, 1915, and 1919, when local families took refuge in the elevated building to escape the rising waters.

Shortly before World War II, a new navigational channel was cut through the marsh, and the lighthouse stood directly in its path. The tower was soon dismantled, but even after a quarter of a century, its screw piles remained so sturdy that they had to be blasted out with dynamite.

REDFISH BAR CUT LIGHTHOUSE

Galveston Bay in Texas

An early-twentieth-century view of the Redfish Bar Cut Lighthouse. Its beacon marked a deepwater channel through the shallows near the middle of Galveston Bay. The old Redfish Bar Lighthouse can be seen in the distance.

ALTHOUGH MANY MILES WIDE, GALVESTON BAY IS ALMOST CUT IN TWO at the middle by Smith Point reaching in from the east and Edwards Point from the west. The shallows of Redfish Bar connect the two points and almost complete the bisection of the bay. Ships crossing the bar on their way to the inner bay and the ports that serve Houston must find the deepest available channel or risk running aground. In 1851 commercial maritime interests paid to have a modest light placed on the bar to mark the deepest passage. Within three years this inadequate, makeshift beacon was replaced by an official government lighthouse. Built on screwpiles, the cottage-style combination dwelling and tower stood directly astride the bar and guided mariners with a sixth-order Fresnel lens. During the Civil War Confederate troops burned the lighthouse to keep it out of Union hands. By 1868 it had been replaced by a second screw-pile structure, which served until about 1900.

Hurricanes and severe gales batter any structure built along the Texas coast, and because of their exposed locations, lighthouses are especially vulnerable. By the turn of the twentieth century, the little lighthouse in Galveston Bay was so beaten up that it was practically falling apart. That same year, a third screw-pile lighthouse was built nearby to mark the deep ship channel the government had recently dredged across the bar. The last coat of paint had barely dried on the white walls of the new lighthouse when the deadly hurricane of 1900 swept over Galveston. Despite a heart-stopping near miss by a huge freighter set adrift by the storm, the station survived. It served until 1936, when it was dismantled and replaced by simple channel lights set on pilings.

LOST LIGHTHOUSES

OF THE WEST

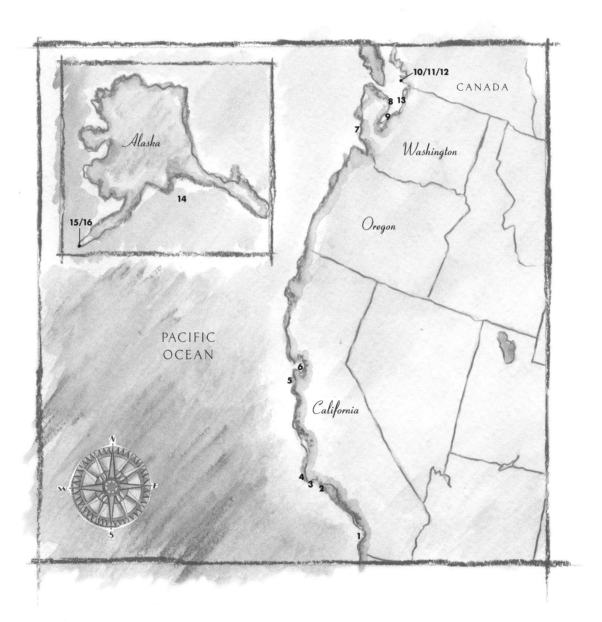

1	Ballast Point	5	Año Nuevo	9	Point Robinson	13	Pulley Point
2	Point Hueneme	6	Alcatraz	10	Smith Island	14	Cape Hinchinbrook
3	Santa Barbara	7	Willapa Bay	11	Patos Island	15	Cape Sarichef
4	Point Arguello	8	Admiralty Head	12	Turn Point	16	Scotch Cap

BALLAST POINT LIGHTHOUSE
San Diego, California

Ballast Point Lighthouse near San Diego shown many years before it was razed to make way for a submarine base. Notice the keeper and his family on the lower left.

IN WAR SUBMARINES HAVE DOOMED MANY FINE SHIPS, BUT RARELY have they claimed a light station. It could be said, however, that the U.S. Navy submarine fleet was responsible for the destruction of one the West's most graceful lighthouses. A two-story, Victorian-style structure built in 1980, the Ballast Point Lighthouse stood beside San Diego Bay for nearly seventy years. Then, in 1960, it was torn down to make way for a new submarine base.

Those persons who love history and attractive architecture regret its loss. Elegant detailing made this tower and attached dwelling a thing of beauty. It was highly functional, too. Its light, focused by a fine fifth-order Fresnel lens, guided countless ships safely into nearby San Diego Harbor. A small automated light still burns on the point, but the beautiful old lighthouse is long gone.

POINT HUENEME LIGHTHOUSE

Oxnard, California

The Point Hueneme Lighthouse during the 1930s. The square tower was more than 50 feet tall, and its light guided ships entering or exiting the Santa Barbara Channel.

A GRACIOUS VICTORIAN BUILDING, THE POINT HUENEME LIGHTHOUSE in Oxnard was a near twin of the Point Fermin Lighthouse in Los Angeles, which still stands. Both structures were completed in 1874 and fitted with matching fourth-order Fresnel lenses. Both stations consisted of an Italianate wooden residence with a square tower rising about 20 feet above their roof lines. The Point Hueneme Station displayed a flashing white light, whereas the Point Fermin Light flashed red.

The Point Heuneme beacon can still be seen, but now it shines from atop a characterless concrete tower. The beautiful old lighthouse was removed shortly before World War II to make way for a major channel-dredging operation. The Coast Guard sold the wooden lighthouse to a local yacht club, which had it barged across the harbor for use as a clubhouse. Eventually, it fell into disrepair and was torn down. The Point Fermin Lighthouse still stands, however, and visitors to Point Fermin Park in Los Angeles can see in it a distant reflection of its vanished sister light at Point Hueneme.

AÑO NUEVO ISLAND LIGHTHOUSE
South of Pigeon Point in California

California's Año Nuevo Island Station as it appeared before the Coast Guard abandoned it in 1948. The hexagonal light tower crests a dune overlooking the fog-signal station.

FOR MANY YEARS THE AÑO NUEVO ISLAND STATION HAD A FOG SIGNAL but no navigational beacon—a light tower was added eventually. The steam-powered fog signal was said to have sounded much like the snort of a bull. With its very first blast during the spring of 1872, the bullish signal stampeded a herd of cows on a nearby dairy farm. Apparently, the fog horn attracted the interest of sea-lion cows as well. On more than one occasion, a herd of blubbery females invaded the station, practically driving the keeper out of his house with their raucous calls and objectionable smells. Except for birds, the sea lions now have the island all to themselves. The facility was abandoned in 1948, and the island was declared a wildlife reserve.

ALCATRAZ ISLAND LIGHTHOUSE
San Francisco, California

The Alcatraz Island Lighthouse in California as it looked during the Civil War only a few years after it was built. Rows of cannonballs stacked in front of the tower and residence give the station a wartime appearance. But it was nature and not war that eventually destroyed the historic, gold-rush-era lighthouse. Severely damaged by the 1906 earthquake that leveled much of San Francisco, it had to be torn down.

THE NAME ALCATRAZ HAS A COLD RING TO IT NOWADAYS, AND NO wonder. For thirty years Alcatraz Island in San Francisco Bay was the site of a notorious federal penitentiary where Al Capone and many other hardened criminals served out their sentences. Even so, mariners and lighthouse lovers have very warm feelings toward this wave-swept rock, for it is home to the oldest major navigational light on the West Coast.

During the early 1850s the U.S. government hired contractor Francis Gibbons to build a small lighthouse on Alcatraz—the name was derived from *alcatraces,* the Spanish word for "pelican." A Cape Cod–style dwelling with a short tower running through its roof, the station was completed and ready for service by June of 1854. Its beacon, focused by a third-order Fresnel lens, lit the way for countless thousands of ships loaded with gold-hungry miners, settlers intent on ranching and farming, or oriental immigrants who came to build railroads, factories, and shops and, along with them, a better life for themselves.

The original Alcatraz Lighthouse appears in a nineteenth-century painting of San Francisco Bay.

Gibbons's lighthouse on "Pelican" Island served well for more than half a century. Then came what Alcatraz keeper B. F. Leeds at first believed was the end of the world. The great earthquake of 1906 destroyed much of old San Francisco and, along with it, the little Alcatraz Island Lighthouse.

The 84-foot, reinforced-concrete tower and adjacent bay-style dwelling that replaced the original lighthouse were destined to share the island with prisons, both military and civilian. As a result, keepers were forced to sleep uncomfortably close to some of the nation's worst bad guys. Ironically, the light was automated and its last keepers removed in 1963, not long before the doors of the Alcatraz Penitentiary, first opened in 1934, slammed shut for the last time. The two-story keeper's residence burned in 1969, but the octagonal tower remains. It is often featured on postcards.

WILLAPA BAY LIGHTHOUSE
North Cove, Washington

The historic Willapa Bay Lighthouse looks peaceful and secure enough in this turn-of-the-twentieth-century view, but eventually it would fall into the Pacific.

AMONG THE FIRST OFFICIAL GOVERNMENT NAVIGATIONAL STATIONS established in the West were those at Smith Island (see page 132) in the Strait of Juan de Fuca and at North Cove near the entrance to Washington's strategic Willapa Bay. Both of these early Pacific lighthouses entered service in October of 1858, and interestingly, both would eventually meet with the same fate—they fell off a cliff. The Willapa Bay Lighthouse stood on a high bluff looking out toward the ocean. Its beacon pointed the way to the relatively calm waters of the bay stretching more than 20 miles to the south and east.

Fitted with a fine Fresnel lens, the Willapa Bay Lighthouse guided mariners for more than eighty years, but by the end of 1940, it had become a "ghost light" in the truest sense. Like the Smith Island Lighthouse far to the north, the combination tower and residence at Willapa Bay was built on unstable ground. Continuously chewing away at the bluff beneath the station, the Pacific had pushed the precipice to within a few feet of the door by 1938. That same year, the station was abandoned, and two years later, it collapsed into the ocean. Along with the lighthouse went much of the town of North Cove. Over the years the Pacific gobbled up 4 square miles of nearby land including streets, homes, stores, hotels, and churches. The community cemetery was saved only because it was moved—caskets, monuments, and all—to a safer location.

These three photographs, taken within months of one another in 1940, document the demise of the Willapa Bay Lighthouse.

ADMIRALTY HEAD LIGHTHOUSE
Whidbey Island, Washington

The original Admiralty Head Lighthouse as it looked at the turn of the twentieth century.

THE PEOPLE OF WHIDBEY ISLAND ARE JUSTIFIABLY PROUD OF THE sparkling white Admiralty Head Lighthouse—one of the most unusual, handsome, and historic structures in Washington State. A two-story brick residence with attached tower, it was completed in 1903. The beacon, focused by its fourth-order Fresnel lens, guided mariners in strategic Admiralty Inlet for almost twenty years. Mostly it served sailing ships, which tended to follow the protected eastern channel through the inlet. This was the age of steam, however, and fewer and fewer coast-hugging schooners visited the inlet, rendering the light unnecessary. In 1922 the Lighthouse Service closed it down and assigned the keeper to other duties. Afterward the U.S. Army took charge of the lighthouse, using it as housing for soldiers stationed at nearby Fort Canby. Abandoned by the military during the 1950s, the dilapidated building was saved from the wrecking ball and restored inside and out to become a key attraction of Fort Canby State Park.

Still standing more than three-quarters of a century after its light last shined, the old lighthouse fascinates park visitors. Many do not realize that an earlier and far more historic lighthouse once marked Admiralty Head. Completed in January of 1861, only months before the outbreak of the Civil War, it was an all-wood building with a square tower rising through its pitched roof. The first keeper was a dauntless seaman who kept Indian war parties at bay with cannon from his ship.

The bright light shining from atop the station's 40-foot tower commanded a 270-degree sweep of the inlet. Windjammer captains approaching Admiralty Inlet from the west depended on the light for guidance, and, no doubt, it saved countless lives. After more than forty years of service, the lighthouse was removed to make way for a gun emplacement at Fort Canby, but that was not the end of its story. After the existing lighthouse entered service in 1903, the old wooden residence was moved back from the cliff and commandeered for use as a barracks for sergeants. About twenty-five years later it was torn down and its timbers used to construct a private residence elsewhere on Whidbey Island.

Built in 1903, but out of service since 1922, this combination residence and tower still stands on Admiralty Head. It is now a popular attraction of Fort Canby State Park.

POINT ROBINSON LIGHTHOUSE

Vashon Island, Washington

NATIONAL ARCHIVES

(Above) The Point Robinson Lighthouse on Washington's Vashon Island still stands and still guides shipping through Puget Sound. The attractive little lighthouse draws many weekend visitors, but few of them know that a much ruder light station once stood here.

(Right) The modest lantern and simple wooden tower of the original Point Robinson Light.

NATIONAL ARCHIVES

SMITH ISLAND LIGHTHOUSE

San Juan Islands, Washington

(Left) A remnant of the shattered Smith Island Lighthouse shares its precarious perch with gulls and cormorants.

(Below) The Smith Island Light Station as it looked in the late nineteenth century.

COAST GUARD MUSEUM NORTHWEST, SEATTLE, WA

NATIONAL ARCHIVES

DURING THE YEARS FOLLOWING THE CALIFORNIA GOLD RUSH, THE U.S. government commissioned sixteen lighthouses and assigned them the formidable task of guarding the nation's entire 2,500-mile western seaboard. Among these valiant and historic sentinels was the Smith Island Lighthouse, completed in 1858. Like many other early western light stations, it consisted of a masonry tower rising from the center of a small, Cape Cod–style dwelling. Focused by a fourth-order Fresnel lens, its beacon marked the far eastern end of the Strait of Juan de Fuca and pointed the way to the Puget Sound.

The stone structure was sturdily built, but almost from the moment the station entered service, its days were numbered. Originally the lighthouse stood more than 200 feet from the island's precipitous cliffs, but over the years, they steadily crumbled away. By the 1950s they had reached the door. With the collapse of the old building imminent, the Coast Guard gave up on it and erected nearby a 45-foot steel-skeleton tower. Soon the lighthouse began to break up and, a little at a time, it fell over the cliff. The last broken timbers vanished during the 1990s.

PATOS ISLAND LIGHTHOUSE

San Juan Islands, Washington

This splendid keeper's residence at the Patos Island Light Station in Washington's San Juan Islands was torn down in 1984. As the two separate families standing on the front porch suggest, the house was a duplex. No doubt, the head keeper lived on one side and his assistant on the other. The walkway on the left led to the wooden light, which still stands. The station was established in 1893.

TURN POINT LIGHTHOUSE
In the San Juan Islands of Washington State

NATIONAL ARCHIVES

The term "lighthouse" seems a bit of an overstatement when applied to the Turn Point Light in Washington State's San Juan Islands. Originally displayed in a simple wooden frame (left), the lantern was placed atop a concrete fog-signal building in 1893. This photograph shows the move actually taking place.

PULLEY POINT LIGHT
Washington State

NATIONAL ARCHIVES

A monument to simplicity, this rude "light tower" on Washington's Pulley Point warned mariners with a railroad-conductor's lantern. Apparently, the builders were so frugal that they resorted to the use of scrap lumber.

CAPE HINCHINBROOK LIGHTHOUSE

Hinchinbrook Island, Alaska

The original Cape Hinchinbrook Lighthouse. Damaged by earthquakes, it was replaced in 1934.

THE CAPE HINCHINBROOK LIGHT GUARDS THE ENTRANCE TO PRINCE William Sound, one of the most beautiful and environmentally sensitive ocean inlets on earth. It also points the way to the port of Valdez, one of the busiest oil ports in the world. So, even today, this beacon remains a vitally important seamark.

The strategic nature of Cape Hinchinbrook was already widely recognized when the first light station was built here in 1909 and 1910. To make sure the lighthouse could do its job and stand up to Alaska's wintry storms, contractor A. B. Lewis and his construction crew of forty men gave it unusually stout walls. The light and fog signal were housed in an octagonal concrete building more than 50 feet in diameter. The lantern room was fitted with a third-order Fresnel lens of an advanced design said to provide the same power as a first-order lens. Shining from an elevation of almost 200 feet, the beacon could be seen from as far as 25 miles at sea. In all the station cost $125,000, a very large sum at the time.

The lighthouse was so solidly built that some people thought it to be "indestructible." However, in 1927 and again in 1928, earthquakes rocked the station, cracking concrete walls, breaking up the foundation, and threatening to dump the entire structure into the Pacific. In 1934 an alarmed Lighthouse Service demolished the structure, replacing it with a new lighthouse built on solid rock. Completed in 1934, the reinforced-concrete structure rises 67 feet above the cliff and displays a powerful light supplied by the station's original third-order lens.

CAPE SARICHEF LIGHTHOUSE

Unimak Island, Alaska

Alaska's Cape Sarichef Lighthouse during the early twentieth century, when it was the most westerly and, perhaps, the loneliest light station in North America.

THE MOST WESTERLY LIGHTHOUSE IN NORTH AMERICA, CAPE SARICHEF Lighthouse clung to bleak Unimak Island, sometimes called the "Roof of Hell" by the Aleuts who lived nearby. Placed here in 1904 to guide ships through the strategic Unimak Pass linking the Bering Sea with the Pacific Ocean, the station could hardly have been more remote. Completely cut off from the outside world, keepers might remain on duty at Cape Sarichef for a year or more at a time. This sort of hard and lonely duty became unnecessary when the station was automated in 1950.

LOST LIGHTHOUSES

OF THE GREAT LAKES

1	Braddock Point	6	Belle Isle	11	Kenosha Pierhead	16	Manitowoc
2	Buffalo	7	Cheboygan	12	Racine Harbor	17	Rawley Point
3	Cleveland	8	De Tour	13	Racine Reef	18	Green Island
4	Turtle Island	9	St. Joseph	14	Root River	19	Long Tail Point
5	West Sister Island	10	Waukegan	15	Port Washington	20	Minnesota Point

BRADDOCK POINT LIGHTHOUSE

Rochester, New York

NATIONAL ARCHIVES

LIGHTHOUSE DIGEST

Now a pleasant lakefront residence, the Braddock Point Lighthouse has been out of service for half a century. The owners have built a lanternlike room on top of the remaining tower walls.

The Braddock Point Lighthouse as it looked early in the twentieth century.

UNLIKE MANY OF THE OTHER "LOST LIGHTS" MENTIONED IN THIS book, the Braddock Point Lighthouse near Rochester, New York, still stands; however, it looks very little like the majestic structure that once marked the western approaches to Rochester's Lake Ontario waterfront. Built during the late 1890s, at the height of the Victorian era, the station's tower soared 110 feet above the water. Seen from many miles out in the lake, it reminded some mariners of an oriental minaret. Focused by a Great Lakes–style Fresnel lens, slightly smaller than a typical third-order coastal lens, its light could be seen from up to 18 miles away.

By the 1950s the building had become ramshackle, and Coast Guard engineers feared the tower might collapse. Consequently, in 1954 the light was extinguished and the top two-thirds of the tower lopped off. The Victorian dwelling and truncated tower now serve as a private residence.

BUFFALO LIGHTHOUSES
Buffalo, New York

The battered Buffalo Breakwater Lighthouse as it looked in 1910.

THE OLD BUFFALO MAIN LIGHTHOUSE, BUILT IN 1833, STILL STANDS AND is a much-honored city landmark. The tower's durability and graceful good looks have won it a place on Buffalo's official city seal. Several other lighthouses, however, brightened the city's busy harbor. One of these, a breakwater lighthouse built in 1872, marked the harbor entrance for almost ninety years.

It is, perhaps, a miracle that the breakwater tower survived for so long since it was repeatedly rammed by heavy freighters and other vessels. From 1899 to 1910 ships slammed the lighthouse no less than four times, doing considerable damage on each occasion. There would be other accidents and close calls, but because the light was badly needed to warn vessels away from the stone breakwater, it was always repaired. Then, in 1958, came the final blow. A large freighter knocked the tower off its foundation causing it to lean out over the water. Soon afterward the building was demolished and replaced by a light on an iron-skeleton tower.

The Buffalo Harbor Lighthouse, another vanished Lake Erie veteran.

The historic 1833 Buffalo Main tower as it looks today.

CLEVELAND LIGHTHOUSE
Cleveland, Ohio

The Cleveland Lighthouse in 1885.

AS A WORK OF ARCHITECTURE, THE HIGH VICTORIAN CLEVELAND Light Station was a standout among American lighthouses. Built in 1872, it replaced an earlier, smaller tower dating back to 1829. The new lighthouse would remain in use for only about twenty years, but it was a truly impressive structure. The huge steep-roofed dwelling, containing two separate residences and nearly twenty rooms, was covered with ornate detailing. The 87-foot octagonal brick tower, rising from a corner of the main building, was reminiscent of the minarets of Byzantium. The lantern room contained a slightly undersized, third-order Fresnel lens of a type designed especially for use on the Great Lakes. The tower stood on a hill, and its light had a focal plane more than 150 feet above the water. The beacon could be seen from more than 18 miles away.

During the early 1890s the station's work of guiding Lake Erie commercial traffic to Cleveland's wharves was taken over by a far less elaborate facility on the breakwater just east of the harbor. To the regret of many people, the magnificent Cleveland Lighthouse was eventually torn down.

TURTLE ISLAND LIGHTHOUSE
Near Toledo, Ohio

(Above) Its steeplelike tower attached to the front of the dwelling, the Turtle Island Lighthouse resembled a church. This photograph dates back to 1890.

(Left) These ruins are all that remain of the station. Even the island, named for an Indian chief named Little Turtle, seems about to disappear.

THE TURTLE ISLAND LIGHT STATION WAS LOCATED SO NEAR THE OHIO-Michigan border that it was never entirely clear which state could claim it. Established in 1832, the station consisted of a two-story brick residence and attached tower. It was rebuilt once in 1866. The Turtle Island beacon guided Lake Erie shipping until 1904, when construction of the Toledo Harbor Lighthouse rendered it obsolete.

WEST SISTER ISLAND LIGHTHOUSE
Western Lake Erie

(Above) Taken about 1859, this antique photograph of the West Sister Island Lighthouse suggests that life was rustic for keepers at the remote station.

(Left) The West Sister Island Light Station as it appeared in 1885.

A DENSE, ALMOST IMPENETRABLE FOREST OF HACKBERRY TREES NOW covers West Sister Island. There has been no dwelling here for decades—the island is an environmentally sensitive wildlife preserve—but this rocky, eighty-five-acre Lake Erie island was home to lighthouse keepers and their families for almost ninety years. Established in 1848, the station consisted of a small conical tower and very modest residence. The people who lived and worked here had to grow their own food and fend for themselves. Usually, children were home-schooled.

The last keeper and his family left the island when the station was automated in 1938. Part of the original tower still stands, but its lantern room has been lopped off. A fully automatic beacon shines in place of the former lamp and Fresnel lens.

BELLE ISLE LIGHTHOUSE
Detroit, Michigan

(Above) Belle Island Lighthouse near Detroit. (Right) Captain Ernest Bondy inspects the fourth-order Fresnel lens at Belle Island Light Station.

FREIGHTERS NAVIGATING THE DETROIT RIVER MUST TAKE CARE TO avoid a 5-square-mile obstacle called Belle Isle. Now an attractive park with a zoo, an aquarium, and a museum, the island was at one time a forbidding marsh overrun with snakes. In fact, the place was known as Snake Island until Detroit's city fathers decided to give it a more lyrical name—having first rooted out the serpents with herds of wild hogs.

Despite its new name the island retained its poisonous reputation among lake sailors, as over the years it claimed more than a few vessels. To help them avoid the island, the U.S. Lighthouse Service established a light station here in 1882. A sturdy, brick Victorian structure, it had a short, square tower on one end of its roof. Focused by a fourth-order Fresnel lens, its light had a focal plane about 40 feet above the water and could be seen from more than 12 miles away. During the years before the Second World War, the lighthouse was demolished to make way for a Coast Guard station.

CHEBOYGAN LIGHTHOUSE
Cheboygan, Michigan

The only known photograph of the Cheboygan Lighthouse, probably taken toward the end of the nineteenth century.

DURING THE NINETEENTH CENTURY MICHIGAN PRODUCED TREMENdous quantities of lumber. Much of it was shipped to markets in the east through small ports such as Cheboygan. Beginning in 1851, the Cheboygan harbor was marked by a lighthouse. Little is known about this early structure except that it fell into disrepair and was torn down in 1859.

That same year a second Cheboygan Lighthouse was completed on the same site. Its 33-foot wooden tower crowned the roof of a two-and-one-half-story dwelling. Fitted with a fifth-order Fresnel lens, it displayed a fixed white light. The station served for more than eighty years before the Coast Guard took it out of service shortly after World War II. Records do not reveal when the lighthouse was torn down, but a former keeper paid his old station a visit in 1947 and found only scattered bricks and rubble.

DE TOUR LIGHTHOUSE
De Tour, Michigan

(Above) The 1861 De Tour skeleton tower and adjacent keeper's residence. The tower was very similar to the one that still marks Whitefish Point on the Upper Michigan Peninsula.

(Right) The De Tour Reef Lighthouse as it looks today. Preservationists are working hard to save the structure.

NOT MUCH IS KNOWN ABOUT THE FIRST LIGHTHOUSE BUILT AT DE Tour, Michigan, in 1848. It was replaced by an 80-foot steel-skeleton tower in 1861, the same year a nearly identical structure was erected at Whitefish Point on Lake Superior. Despite its height and, for its time, quite modern appearance, the steel giant could do little to protect lake sailors from dangerous De Tour Reef, located some distance from shore. More than a few vessels came to grief on the reef's jagged rocks. In 1931 De Tour Reef finally received a lighthouse of its own, built on a massive concrete base. This made the old, 1861 De Tour Lighthouse redundant, and it was torn down.

ST. JOSEPH LIGHTHOUSE
St. Joseph, Michigan

(Above) The St. Joseph Pier Lights were featured on a postage stamp. Unlike the main St. Joseph Light Station in town, they still stand.

(Right) Almost a century old, the historic St. Joseph Lighthouse was leveled in 1954 to make room for a parking lot. Too many of America's historic structures have suffered the same sorry fate.

DURING THE EARLY 1990s THE U.S. POSTAL Service featured the St. Joseph Pier Lights in its series of stamps celebrating America's historic lighthouses. A lovely pair of range light towers, they rise directly from the deep blue waters of Lake Michigan and, of course, look great on an envelope. Philatelists, however, may not be aware that an equally attractive and even more historic lighthouse once served St. Joseph. Built in 1859 on a hill above the harbor, this stately structure consisted of a nicely detailed two-story residence crested by a tower and lantern.

When the range lights—among the first in the nation—were completed in 1907, lighthouse officials planned to extinguish the "beacon on the hill." The captains of lake freighters objected, and the original station remained in operation until 1924. After its retirement as an active lighthouse, the building served for many years as local headquarters for the American Red Cross. In 1954 it was sold to the city and, despite the outcry of preservationists, was torn down to make way for a parking lot.

WAUKEGAN LIGHTHOUSE
Waukegan, Illinois

John Williams, a one-armed Civil War hero, maintained this lighthouse in Waukegan, Illinois, for twenty-seven years.

AT THE END OF A BREAKWATER IN WAUKEGAN, ILLINOIS, ABOUT 30 MILES north of Chicago, an automated light shines from the top of the stubby iron cylinder—all that remains of what was at one time a fine Lake Michigan light station. In all, three different lighthouses have served this busy midwestern port. The first, a small brick structure, was built in 1847. The second, consisting of a modest wooden residence and tower, was completed in 1860 just as the nation descended into the political chaos that led to the Civil War.

The station's best-known keeper was a one-armed Civil War veteran named John Williams, who received his appointment from Abraham Lincoln in March of 1865. By the time Williams had moved into the keeper's residence that same May, the president who had hired him had been assassinated. But Williams, who had lost an arm at the Battle of Gettysburg, remained faithful to his appointment. He and his wife, Helen, raised seven children at the station, and he tended the light until the day he died in February 1892.

In 1899 the Civil War–era station was razed, and a new lighthouse was built at the end of the harbor's long breakwater. The pier lighthouse served until 1967, when a mysterious fire gutted the building. Afterward, a Coast Guard wrecking crew knocked down the ruins, leaving only a portion of the tower.

An antique postcard features the Waukegan Breakwater Lighthouse.

The Waukegan Breakwater Station besieged by ice in 1913.

KENOSHA PIERHEAD LIGHTHOUSES

Kenosha, Wisconsin

871. Lighthouses at entrance of Harbor, Kenosha, Wis.

NATIONAL ARCHIVES

Heavily outlined and tinted, this antique postcard view of the Kenosha Pierhead Lights looks almost like a painting. The strange, almost rocketlike tower on the left dates back to the 1860s. Unfortunately, it was removed long ago. The more conventional tower on the right still stands, and it has been painted bright red.

LIGHTHOUSE DIGEST

RACINE HARBOR LIGHTHOUSE

Racine, Wisconsin

Waves pound the Racine Pier and its lighthouse. This photograph was likely taken shortly before World War I.

DURING THE LATE 1840s THE CITY GOVERNMENT OF RACINE BUILT piers at the end of the Root River to attract commerce. A small light was installed at the end of the northernmost pier to alert mariners approaching the city from Lake Michigan. In 1859 the schooner *Newman* failed to heed the warning, slammed into the pier, and carried away the light. Several years and the Civil War would pass before a new light was established here. Completed in 1866, it shined from a small stone building, which doubled as a harbor-patrol office. Although made redundant by the Wind Point Lighthouse, built in 1880, the harbor beacon remained in use until about 1918. The Wind Point Station, with its soaring 108-foot tower, is still in operation.

RACINE REEF LIGHTHOUSE
Racine, Wisconsin

The Racine Reef Light Station as it looked about 1907. Note the pointy ice breaks protruding from the foundation. The concrete base was sheathed in copper to protect it from wave action.

AMONG THE MORE REMARKABLE ghost lights of the Great Lakes mentioned in this book is the historic Racine Reef Lighthouse, built in 1906 and demolished in 1961. This unusual lighthouse is fondly remembered by Lake Michigan sailors, some of whom may have owed their lives to its guidance. The beacon warned vessels away from a ship-killing obstacle about 2 miles offshore from Racine, Wisconsin. An earlier lighthouse had marked the Racine Reef from 1850 until shortly before the turn of the twentieth century, when it was torn down. By 1906 it had been replaced by a brick-and-iron structure placed on a heavy concrete foundation rising 17 feet out of the water. Built on this solid platform was a unique, Victorian-style residence with an octagonal tower sweeping upward from its pointed roof. Constantly manned by a two-man crew, the station remained in service until 1954, when the light was automated. The Coast Guard demolished the building in 1961.

The Racine Reef Lighthouse being demolished in 1961.

ROOT RIVER LIGHTHOUSE
Racine, Wisconsin

There are no known photographs of the Root River Lighthouse that at one time marked the harbor of Racine, Wisconsin. This sketch was made in 1912 by an artist working from descriptions provided by local residents who had seen the old station.

NO ONE ALIVE TODAY REMEMBERS THE ROOT RIVER LIGHTHOUSE THAT in the past guided ships into the port of Racine, Wisconsin. It stood near the present site of the Racine Public Library. Established in 1839, the station served until it was discontinued in 1865, at the end of the American Civil War. Built by a local brick manufacturer, no doubt using his own product, the tower had brick walls nearly 3 feet thick. Both the tower and dwelling were torn down in 1876 to provide materials for a private residence.

PORT WASHINGTON LIGHTHOUSE

Port Washington, Wisconsin

A 1927 view of the Port Washington Lighthouse. The lantern was removed after construction of a light tower at the end of a nearby breakwater.

ESTABLISHED IN 1860, THE SAME YEAR ABRAHAM LINCOLN WAS ELECTED president, the Port Washington Light marked a small but busy harbor and port to the north of Milwaukee. The tower stood atop a two-story keeper's residence built on a bluff well back from Lake Michigan. During the early 1930s the government built a lengthy breakwater to protect the harbor from storm-generated waves. In 1934 a light tower was placed at the end of the breakwater, and the original Port Washington Light Station became obsolete. Although the tower was removed from its roof long ago, the original keeper's residence still stands in the heart of the Port Washington business district.

MANITOWOC LIGHTHOUSES

Manitowoc, Wisconsin

(Above) The port city of Manitowoc, Wisconsin, was once served by a pair of lighthouses. The brick lighthouse seen above stood on a hilltop overlooking the mouth of the Manitowoc River. Built in 1840, it was torn down shortly before the turn of the twentieth century.

(Right) The second Manitowoc beacon was a pierhead light, which guided vessels to the city's wharves. Established during the 1850s, the pierhead station remained in service for more than ninety years.

RAWLEY POINT LIGHTHOUSE
Two Rivers, Wisconsin

No photographs of the original Rawley Point Lighthouse are known to exist. This remarkable painting done by one of the station's assistant keepers gives an idea of what it looked like.

NOW MORE THAN A CENTURY OLD, A REMARKABLY MODERN-LOOKING steel tower soars above Wisconsin's Rawley Point on the western shore of Lake Michigan. The skeleton tower was moved here from Chicago, where, along with the world's first giant Ferris wheel, it helped attract throngs to the 1893 Columbian Exposition. After the fair the tower was taken apart, piece by piece, and shipped north to Rawley Point, where it still guides mariners and draws its share of wide-eyed visitors.

Visitors who come to see the lighthouse and enjoy the natural wonders of nearby Point Beach State Forest may not be aware that several earlier light towers formerly guarded these shores. Among them was a temporary light consisting of a lantern held aloft by several 75-foot-long poles. This makeshift coast mark was replaced during the 1850s by a true lighthouse with a frame tower and keeper's residence. In 1873 this wooden lighthouse gave way to a much more impressive brick structure. Attached to its spacious dwelling was a brick tower, about 80 feet tall. The iron lantern at the top held a third-order Fresnel lens. The upper portion of the brick tower was removed after its taller modern replacement arrived from Chicago in 1894.

GREEN ISLAND LIGHTHOUSE
Near Marinette, Wisconsin

U.S. COAST GUARD

(Above) The spacious Green Island Lighthouse provided keepers and their families with a comfortable home as well as a job. An interior staircase led to the lantern room. Abandoned during the 1930s, the station fell into ruin.

(Right) Frank Drew grew up at the remote Green Island Light Station where his father was keeper. When his parents died in 1882, Drew left to pilot and captain commercial vessels plying the Great Lakes. In 1909, after a seventeen-year absence, he returned to take over as keeper of the same lighthouse he had lived in as a boy.

U.S. COAST GUARD

FOR MUCH OF ITS MORE THAN HALF CENTURY OF SERVICE, THE GREEN Island Lighthouse in Lake Michigan's Green Bay was kept by members of a single Wisconsin family. During the late 1860s career Lighthouse Service man Samuel Drew became keeper of this isolated island station, located several miles offshore from Marinette, Wisconsin. The keeper's son, Frank Drew, grew up on Green Island and eventually took over as keeper of the station.

The Drew family witnessed one of the nation's worst natural disasters and kept the Green Island light burning through it all. During the summer of 1871, when the great Pestigo fire obliterated whole towns and consumed entire forests on the nearby Wisconsin mainland, Green Island was blanketed by smoke for days. Seeing the bright flames and black smoke in the distance, the Drews at first wondered if the world was coming to an end and turned to their family Bible for solace. The billowing black smoke eventually became so dense that the light was kept burning even during daylight hours.

LONG TAIL POINT LIGHTHOUSE
Suamico, Wisconsin

The Long Tail Point Lighthouse and the old 1849 tower as seen from a passing vessel.

NEAR THE LOWER END OF WISCONSIN'S GREEN BAY, NOT FAR FROM the city of the same name, a long, narrow point of land extends southeasterly into its blue-green water. On a map this peninsula resembles the flowing tail of a horse, and so it was named Long Tail Point. Its colorful name is not the only thing remarkable about the point.

It was formerly the site of three different lighthouses. At one time all three were standing. Now all three are gone.

The first tower was built here in 1849 on orders of Stephen J. Pleasonton, the Treasury Department autocrat who governed the U.S. "Lighthouse Establishment" for more than thirty years. Pleasonton was widely known as a penny-pincher, and his tightfisted-

A closer view of the second light. An attempt to move the building failed when it broke through the ice and sank in the waters of Green Bay.

ness showed through in the construction of the Long Tail Point Station. Laborers used unquarried stone, much of it gathered along the shore, to build the 5-foot-thick walls of the tower. The site was neither carefully selected nor adequately protected from erosion. By 1859, some years after Pleasonton had lost his grip on America's lighthouses, government inspectors concluded that the tower would soon collapse. It was abandoned, and another lighthouse was built nearby

The second Long Tail Point Lighthouse consisted of a two-story, wooden keeper's dwelling with a short, square tower positioned on its roof. To better serve freighters running in fog, a third lighthouse was built in the water just off the point shortly before the turn of the century. Its keepers, however, continued to live in the old residence onshore.

After the station was automated in 1936, the residence was sold to a private owner who attempted to trailer it across the winter ice to a new location. The heavy building broke through the ice and was crushed. A few of its timbers were salvaged for construction of a nearby farm silo. In 1973 the station's third tower was blown off its open-water pier by a storm, and it, too, was destroyed. Ironically, all that remains of the Long Tail Point Light Station is the ruin of the original stone tower, still standing more than 140 years after inspectors pronounced its doom.

This third tower was washed into Green Bay by a storm in 1973.

MINNESOTA POINT LIGHTHOUSE

Near Duluth, Minnesota

This rather ramshackle-looking light station near Duluth guided ships on Lake Superior from 1858 until 1885, when it was permanently closed. The photograph dates back to 1870.

All that remains of the Minnesota Point Lighthouse is the weathered stump of its tower.

A BELL FOR THE KEEPERS

THE GHOST SHIPS OF POINT ARGUELLO

U.S. Navy Captain Edward Watson had never seen a fog as thick as the one that shrouded the California coast on the evening of September 8, 1923. Captain Watson was in overall command of a sizable flotilla of fourteen destroyers steaming southward from San Francisco enroute to the large navy base at San Diego. The destroyers had completed about half their journey and soon would be making a wide eastward turn around Points Arguello and Conception—or so Captain Watson believed. In vain he peered into the dense fog, hoping to catch a glimpse of lighthouse beacons calling to him from these strategic points of land. Once he had them in view, he knew his ships could safely turn to port and enter the protected waters of the Santa Barbara Channel. But on this fateful night, he would never see the lights.

Maintaining a precise military formation, the destroyers ran one behind the other about two minutes apart. Their nervous skippers waited for Captain Watson to give the order to change course. A navy veteran with many years of service, Watson was a decisive commander, but tonight, in this fog, he was hesitant. His radioman had received a confusing electronic signal from Point Arguello. The radio beacon indicated that Captain Watson's lead ship, the *Delphy,* was still north of the point. If this were true, then what lay to the east was not the safe water of the Santa Barbara Channel, but rather a solid wall of ship-killing rocks.

There had been a second, conflicting radio signal received that night—one indicating that the flotilla was, indeed, about to enter the channel. Captain Watson weighed the informa-

NATIONAL ARCHIVES

The Point Arguello Lighthouse as it looked in 1902, only about a year after it entered service. Perched on a cliff, the square tower was just 28 feet high. The lantern room contained a fourth-order Fresnel lens.

tion he had received and made a fateful decision. He would ignore both radio signals and rely on an old sailor's gut instincts. Navigating by dead reckoning, he plotted the flotilla's position and course. Then he gave his ships their orders, and, one by one, they turned to port.

As it happened, Captain Watson's instincts had failed him, and his flotilla was still far from the channel. The screams of metal—and men—could be heard as the *Delphy* struck the coast at a place called Honda, about a mile north of Point Arguello. Then, one after another, six more destroyers—the *Lee,* the *Young,* the *Woodbury,* the *Chauncey,* the *Nicholas,* and the

Fuller—followed the *Delphy* to their doom. The other ships in the flotilla managed to bear off in time to save themselves, but the seven at the head of the column were lost. Grinding to a halt on the rocks, they were soon torn apart by the pounding surf. In all, twenty-three sailors would be killed in the mishap. The toll might have been much higher if not for the rescue efforts organized by keepers from the Point Arguello Lighthouse.

Keepers Gotford Olson, Arvel Settles, and Jesse Mygrants had heard the droning engines of the destroyers as they steamed toward the rocks. What lay ahead for these three Lighthouse Service veterans was a hellish night filled with the screech of steel on stone, exploding boilers, and the cries of drowning men. There had been nothing they could do to prevent the calamity, but once it had happened, they swung into action. Plunging into the boiling surf off Honda, they dragged one after another shipwrecked sailor to safety. Injured men were littered to the lighthouse, where they were bandaged and sheltered. Coffee, food, and medicine were brought down from the light station on the cliffs to the beaches below, where stunned seamen huddled in small groups. The keepers kept it up all night and into the next day.

Having risked their lives to save and comfort so many, all three keepers received official commendations from the U.S. Navy. These would be their only rewards—except for the satisfaction of having done their duty. Within a few days after the incident, they had settled back into their lonely routines at the Point Arguello Lighthouse. Eventually, an anchor was placed on the nearby cliffs to serve as a memorial for the men who died at Honda. There is no separate monument dedicated to Olson, Settles, and Mygrants. Even the lighthouse where they lived and worked is now gone.

The Point Arguello Light Station was established in 1901 on a barren cliff almost 100 feet above the Pacific waves. Its beacon helped mark the strategic rocky elbow where California's generally north/south trending coastline angles sharply back toward the east.

Four U.S. Navy destroyers lay wrecked at Honda, just north of the Point Arguello Lighthouse. Commanded by skippers who thought they were heading into the Santa Barbara Channel, these and three other ships not seen in this photograph steamed right up onto the rocks. This disaster in 1923 cost the lives of nearly two dozen sailors.

Exposed and isolated, the lighthouse was never a popular duty station for keepers, and it remained in operation only until 1934, when it was replaced by an automated light on an iron-skeleton tower. Shortly after it was decommissioned, the old tower and residence was razed. Like Captain Watson's ill-fated flotilla, it is now only a ghostly memory.

FALLING OFF THE ROOF OF HELL

Lighthouse keepers often risked their lives in the line of duty. More than a few not only risked their lives but *lost* them. Some were killed while attempting daring rescues like those at Honda in 1923. Others died in falls, fires, or explosions. Still others perished in hurricanes or nor'easters that swept away entire light stations. For the five keepers serving at Alaska's Scotch Cap Lighthouse in 1946, death came like a winged monster from the deep, with the speed of a jet plane and a force that no structure of steel and stone could have resisted.

No light station in America—or in all the world, for that matter—was more isolated than the one at Scotch Cap on Unimak Island in the Aleutians. Completed and placed in service in 1903, it guided vessels through the narrow passage linking the open Pacific Ocean with the Bering Sea. Believing the island to be haunted, Aleutian natives referred to it as "the Roof of Hell," but the lighthouse keepers at Scotch Cap tended to think of it as "the end of the earth."

Unimak Island was so remote that, during the early part of the century, lighthouse tenders visited it only once a year at most. Keepers served at the Scotch Cap Station for up to three years and then were given a year of leave to help them reestablish their ties with the outside world. Once the Coast Guard took custody of America's lighthouses, tours of duty at Scotch Cap and other such isolated stations were limited to one year. Even so, a year can be a very long time in a place where seals and polar bears are your only neighbors.

For Jack Colvin, Paul Ness, Leonard Pickering, Anthony Pettit, and Dewey Dykstra, five young Coast Guardsmen posted here just after World War II, their year on Unimak would become an eternity. Only one of the five—no one knows which—was awake, keeping watch over the vital Scotch Cap Light, when an earthquake struck shortly after 1:30 A.M. on April 1, 1946. No doubt the shock tumbled the other four keepers out of their beds, and they soon joined their on-duty comrade to check the station. The Scotch Cap Lighthouse was solidly built, so they likely found only a little damage—some broken dishes, displaced equipment, open cabinets and lockers, and that sort of thing. But no one was about to go back to bed. Something strange was happening out there in the ocean. Water was draining away from the island and rushing out toward the Pacific. Shortly after 2:15 that morning they saw what had happened to

With walls of concrete and steel, the remote Scotch Cap Lighthouse on Unimak Island in Alaska was built to resist the earthquakes and fierce storms that plague this region. No matter how sturdy its construction, however, the station could not have survived the 100-foot-high tidal wave that hit it in 1946. The building was crushed and washed into the sea along with its five keepers.

all that water. It had been sucked up into a tidal wave, at least 100 feet high, and it was flying toward them at 500 miles per hour. There was no escape.

According to the crew of a direction finding station located far up on the Unimak Island cliffs, the tsunami struck the lighthouse at 2:18 A.M. By the time the sea had calmed, the foundation of the reinforced-concrete building was all that was left of the Scotch Cap Light Station. The crew of the direction-finding station survived the disaster and eventually located the bodies of the five keepers after they washed up on the shore of Unimak Island. A small memorial on the site of the original Scotch Cap Lighthouse honors the victims of the 1946 earthquake and tidal wave.

KEEP THE LIGHT BURNING

Lighthouse keeping has always been hazardous work. America's first lighthouse keeper was a man named George Worthylake, who took charge of the stone tower on Boston's Little Brewster Island shortly after it was completed in 1716. A part-time harbor pilot and shepherd with a large family, Worthylake survived the job for only about a year. He drowned in a boating accident while on the way back from the mainland, where he gone to collect the small salary paid him for lighting the station's tallow candles each evening.. Robert Saunders, the man who replaced Worthylake, also drowned not long after he was hired. The profession of lighthouse keeping had gotten off to an ominous start in America.

Fortunately, there have always been brave men and women willing to keep the lights burning. Thanks to their dedication over the centuries, the nation's ports have prospered, and uncounted thousands of ships and lives have been saved. Most keepers' stories have ended more happily than those of Worthylake and Saunders—but not always.

One of the worst and most dramatic lighthouse tragedies struck only a few miles south of the Boston Light. There, not far from the town of Cohasset, a deadly shoal lurks just beneath the surface of Massachusetts Bay, waiting to destroy any ship that ventures too near. Over the years this shoal, known as Minots Ledge, exacted a ghastly toll of barks, brigs, coasters, ketches, schooners, and large ships along with a large number of passengers and crew. It was long thought impossible to mark the ledge with a light.

Urged on by increasing losses in vessels and lives, U.S. lighthouse officials finally made an attempt to mark Minots in 1847. A young engineer named I.W.P. Lewis argued that a

This sketch shows the Minots Ledge skeleton tower as it looked before its collapse in 1851. Two assistant keepers were killed in the disaster. A memorial to honor the memory of the two keepers is now being built in Cohasset, Massachusetts.

lighthouse could be built in open water directly over the ledge. Unlike most light towers of the time, which were mostly stone or brick cylinders, this one would consist of an elevated dwelling and lantern placed on top of several long, heavily braced iron legs. In theory the skeletal structure would allow storm winds and large waves to pass right through without doing harm.

The Lighthouse Service adopted the Lewis scheme, and by New Year's Day in 1850, the experimental light station became operational. For better than a year, all went well. The full-time three-man crew lit the station lamps every night, and mariners were happy to have the Minots beacon to warn them away from the ship-killing ledge. But when storms swept in from the Atlantic, the crew noticed an uncomfortable swaying motion as large waves slammed into the tower.

On the night of March 16–17, 1851, an especially powerful gale descended on coastal Massachusetts. As it happened, head keeper John Bennett was ashore on leave when the storm hit. He had left the station in the capable hands of his assistants, Joseph Wilson and Joseph Antoine, whom he knew would keep the light burning, no matter what happened. As the intensity of the storm increased, however, Bennett began to fear for the safety of his friends in the Minots tower. He was right to be worried.

Huge, rolling waves pounded the tower incessantly. At some point on the afternoon of March 17, the steel skeleton lurched and began to lean. With each passing wave the lean grew worse until, at last, the tower could take no more, and it fell into the ocean. The bodies of Wilson and Antoine later washed up onshore. Keeper Bennett noted with considerable pride that his crewmen had kept the light burning right up to the end. Those who witnessed the disaster say the station bell rang out wildly as the last waves swept over the tower.

After the catastrophic failure of the original open-skeleton design, Congress funded the construction of a stone tower to mark Massachusetts's deadly Minots Ledge. Completed shortly before the Civil War, the granite tower still stands, and its light remains in service.

LIGHTHOUSE DIGEST

ANCIENT BELLS AND GHOSTLY LIGHTS

Much like the ships and sailors who have depended on them for so many centuries, lighthouses are perishable. As we have seen, many of our nation's earliest lighthouses disappeared long ago. Storms bowled them over or floods washed away their foundations, causing them to fall into the sea. A few were blasted by cannonballs, kegs of gunpowder, or other weapons of war. Many fell to the same people who had built them in the first place—members of the Lighthouse Service or Coast Guard, who pulled them down to make room for newer, supposedly better navigational facilities. Many others simply grew old, crumbled, and collapsed.

Whenever a lighthouse is destroyed, America loses a valuable link with its past, a reminder of the often-heroic struggles of mariners and the men and women who worked night and day to keep the lights burning. Fortunately, not all fallen lighthouses are lost forever. In some cases parks, local governments, or preservationist groups have rebuilt fallen towers for use as monuments or museums. Others live on in memory. Some old salts swear that when the sun sets on a hazy summer evening, they can still see the faint signal of a long-ago extinguished navigational beacon and even hear the call of its bell.

The next time you walk along a beach at nightfall, listen carefully and scan the horizon. Who knows what ancient bells you may hear or ghostly lights you may see?

LIGHTHOUSE DIGEST ARCHIVES

Although far from our shores and long ago destroyed, this burned-out light tower speaks eloquently of the bravery and perseverance of Americans. Built by the Spanish in 1897 on top of Corregidor Island in the Philippines, it once guided ships into Manila Bay. The lighthouse was all but destroyed during the lengthy World War II Japanese siege of Corregidor and when U.S. forces retook the island fortress in 1945. The base and bricks of the tower were used to build a new lighthouse of similar design, which now serves as a memorial to those who lost their lives in the battles at Corregidor.

INDEX OF LIGHTHOUSES

LIGHTHOUSE PRESERVATION SOCIETIES

American Lighthouse Foundation
P.O. Box 889
Wells, Maine 04090–0889

U.S. Lighthouse Society
244 Kearney Street, 5th floor
San Francisco, CA 94108

Great Lakes Lighthouse Keepers Association
c/o Henry Ford Estate
4901 Evergreen Road
Dearborn, MI 48128–2406

New Jersey Lighthouse Society
P.O. Box 4228
Brick, NJ 08723

Outer Banks Lighthouse Society
302 Driftwood Street
Nags Head, NC 27959

Florida Lighthouse Association
4931 South Peninsula Drive
Ponce Inlet, FL 32127

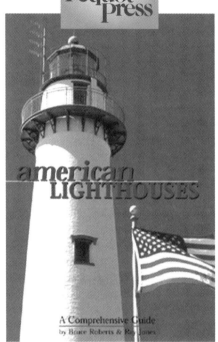